Transformative Mindfulness in Education

Learn how to support your wellness while you're engaging in social justice change work in schools and classrooms.

Mindfulness practices support our well-being and our capacity to navigate the challenges that are common when trying to support change. Throughout the book, you will find mindfulness practices to build self-awareness and guidance to identify injustices within your setting. You'll also gain strategies for building collaborative teams and groups through generative conflict, developing community agreements, and learning how to repair so that change can be sustained.

Bonus: Audio recordings of some of the guided practices are available on the book's product page on Routledge.com to support your experience.

Rhiannon Kim, Ed.D., CGS-RBA, M.S. CCC-SLP, E-RYT 200, RYT 500, has worked within the public education system in various roles for 18 years. She has taught graduate-level courses to future educators and current educators as an adjunct lecturer and has facilitated professional development centered on mindfulness, implicit bias, trauma and trauma-informed practices, and anti-oppressive practices with educators, future educators, and mental health service providers for over 11 years. She has taught meditation and yoga for nearly 15 years, and her methods are rooted in anti-oppressive and healing-centered practices.

Equity and Social Justice in Education Series

Paul C. Gorski, Series Editor

Routledge's Equity and Social Justice in Education series is a publishing home for books that apply critical and transformative equity and social justice theories to the work of on-the-ground educators. Books in the series describe meaningful solutions to the racism, white supremacy, economic injustice, sexism, heterosexism, transphobia, ableism, neoliberalism, and other oppressive conditions that pervade schools and school districts.

Latina Pedagogies of Care
How Cariño Can Give Tired Teachers Power and Hope
Ale Babino and Rocío Almanza

Abolition in School Counseling
Practicing Liberation and Community in PK-12 Schools
Riley Drake and Alicia Oglesby

Navigating Power, Harnessing Possibility
A Guide for Leading Schools Through Uncertain Times
Mary Rice-Boothe

Community, Love, and Connection in Early Care and Education
An Interactive Guide for Holistic, Equitable Early Learning
Meghan L. Green, Lilly Padia, and Mariana Souto-Manning

Transformative Mindfulness in Education
Caring for Ourselves While Kindling Change
Rhiannon Kim

Teaching Indigenous Studies
An Introduction for K-12 Educators
Leilani Sabzalian, Meredith McCoy, and Helen Thomas

Transformative Mindfulness in Education

Caring for Ourselves While Kindling Change

Rhiannon Kim

NEW YORK AND LONDON

Designed cover image: Getty Images

First published 2027
by Routledge
605 Third Avenue, New York, NY 10158

and by Routledge
4 Park Square, Milton Park, Abingdon, Oxon, OX14 4RN

Routledge is an imprint of the Taylor & Francis Group, an informa business

ISBN: 978-1-032-87117-2 (pbk)
ISBN: 978-1-003-54068-7 (ebk)

DOI: 10.4324/9781003540687

Typeset in Palatino
by SPi Technologies India Pvt Ltd (Straive)

Access the Support Material: www.routledge.com/9781032871172

To everyone who was afraid they didn't matter.
You matter more than you know.

Contents

Acknowledgements viii

Introduction 1

1 **Mindfulness: Learning to Be in the Moment** 6

2 **Applied and Relational Mindfulness Practices** 22

3 **Beginning to Explore Our Emotional Landscape** 34

4 **Exploring Social Identities** 51

5 **Identifying Our Values** 61

6 **Are We Well?** 67

7 **Reflecting on Power in the System** 86

8 **Identifying Bias in Our Schools** 99

9 **The Impact of Biased Perceptions of Emotions** 116

10 **Addressing Control in Schools** 132

11 **Creating a Culture to Engage in Collaborative Changework** 147

12 **Engaging in Generative Conflict** 163

13 **Relational Repair Work** 177

14 **We Are the Changemakers** 192

Appendix: Notes on Introducing Mindfulness to Others 206

References 211

Acknowledgements

I owe a debt of gratitude to many people who supported me in this process.

I am ever-grateful to the youth I have had the privilege of knowing and learning from. I am also deeply grateful to the many educators I have had the honor of learning alongside, as a colleague, in courses, as a consultant, and within friendships.

To my entire family, who beams with pride and joy about the work that went into creating this book and the book itself; thank you for believing in me and for your love. Thank you to my nieces, who teach me how to enjoy the moment and embody love, play, silliness, and joy all the time.

I am ever grateful to my friend and Conscious Homestead founder, Candace, and the entire crew there who show up in ways our world needs so much more of: building a community with foundations of mutuality, collaboration, community care, love, joy, and wholeness. Thank you to Sara, Amanda, and Jessie for your steady support on my healing journey.

Dolan! Oh, Dolan. I literally could not have done this without you. You are the best in so many ways. Thank you for your editing prowess and all-around amazingness. Thank you to my editors, Lauren and Paul, for your steady support and believing in my work.

Thank you to my Nurturing the Nurturers co-creators, Addison, Alex, and Arlène, for teaching me what a lovingly collaborative space can be and feels like.

To my elders: Thank you to my Grandparents for your unconditional and unwavering love; your confidence in me has helped me in innumerable ways. Thank you to Mamaw and Pop for your love and kindness to me always. Thank you to 할머니 for your courage and strength and to you and Alan for your love and support.

To my partner, Brian, my love and one of my best teachers: thank you for challenging me and being willing to be challenged by me. I continue to transform, heal, and grow so much in our partnership. Thank you, I love you.

Introduction

Thank you for choosing this book. I wrote this in hopes that the offerings in here will serve as part of your healing work toward justice.

My pronouns are she|her|hers. I am mixed-race Asian (Korean) and White. I am second generation Korean American on my father's side and of mixed White European ancestry on my mother's side. I identify as racially and ethnically ambiguous and as a Person of Color. There are people who have similar lineages and physical presentations who do not use the term *ambiguous*. This is a self-claimed term. It emerged from the reality that, depending on who is perceiving me, I am viewed as Mixed, Asian, Latine, White, Indigenous, or *other*.

Writing this book is a culmination of reflecting on my experiences as a mixed-race Korean and White child and student who went through public education in one of the whitest states in the U.S. and then worked within the public education system in various roles, not including internships in graduate school, for 18 years. I worked as a para educator, a 1:1 interventionist, a K-5 speech language pathologist (SLP), a summer school preK SLP, as an interdisciplinary team member consulting across a school district from preschool through 12th grade, and as a consultant.

I have taught courses to future educators and current educators in my role as an adjunct lecturer in addition to facilitating professional development centered on mindfulness, implicit bias, trauma and trauma-informed practices and anti-oppressive practices with educators, future educators, and mental health service providers for over a decade.

I hold an EdD in Educational Leadership and Policy Studies with a Certificate of Graduate Study in Resiliency-Based Approaches (CGS-RBA) from the University of Vermont. My dissertation focused on the impact of a pedagogy I experimented and developed over the past 11 years of working as an

DOI: 10.4324/9781003540687-1

adjunct lecturer and facilitator entitled *Exploring the Impact of an Embodied Socially Just Healing Pedagogy of Praxis: A Mixed Methods Study* (2023). I also hold a Bachelor's Degree with a dual major of Communication Sciences and Disorders and Psychology, and a Master's of Science in Communication Disorders and Sciences.

All these experiences, the observations of classrooms, hallways, the playground, the cafeteria, of the ways special education does and doesn't fulfill its potential to support disabled youth, the conversations with youth, with families, and with people working within a dysfunctional system have influenced the pages that follow. This book uses examples that are not from any particular setting, but are a composite of many different settings, conversations, and observations across educational institutions and other organizations. There are also personal experiences that have been de-identified.

This book seeks to address both the internal work of engaging in self-reflection as to how we may unknowingly be upholding the systems that are harming us and the external work of examining the ways systems organized around power over, domination, and hierarchy are creating dis-ease for so many of us. We need to look inward and outward and engage in change work that is both internal and external.

This book will not provide you with ways to teach students resilience or other techniques to manage behavior. It was written with a focus on building wellness, deeper awareness, and ways to navigate the complicated and beautiful world of education.

Mindfulness practices such as meditation and yoga continue to anchor me and connect me to myself, other people and the broader world. Mindfulness practices are most potent when they are used to increase our capacity to be fully present, learn to be with discomfort, to be honest, and to accept what is (the good, the bad, and the neutral). Some mindfulness practices stop with that. However, we also need to use that presence and awareness to then make conscious choices that benefit both ourselves and others.

We live in a world that prioritizes urgency and perfectionism across all aspects of our lives. For educators, this means learning the brand-new curriculum that is rolled out each time there is a change in leadership - both of which seem to happen every other school year. There is pressure not just to learn the new materials, sequence, and language but also to do it with "fidelity," which is actually code for "perfectly." Standards are set by people far removed from work with students, with lofty goals such as "all students will be reading on grade level by the end of next school year.". Meanwhile, public education funding continues to be scrutinized while there always seems to be a surplus of funds available to support war, and the public opinion of educators in the United States continues to devalue and undercut the important role schools - and, most importantly, educators - play in enhancing and transforming our world for the better.

With this in mind, I wrote this book with the hope that you can take this and engage with the content slowly and with intentionality. It is not something to read as quickly as you need to eat your lunch during your so-called *lunch break* while calling families and grading assignments students turned in last week.

I will invite you to pause and reflect throughout the book. It may be helpful to have a designated journal to keep your reflections in as they will build upon each other throughout the book. These pauses to reflect are practices of mindfulness. There are many schools of thought and various teachings on mindfulness across cultures.

Over the past two decades, I have learned from many people about different approaches to mindfulness. Some teachers focused on mindfulness as being synonymous with calmness. Yet this approach can stifle and suppress natural emotions (more on this in Chapter 1), and can even be weaponized in schools trying to coerce students and educators into being "mindful," which actually becomes coded language for "compliant." Mindfulness can support us in moving toward calmness, but mindfulness is not about being perpetually calm. It is not a practice to numb our senses; rather it is one to hone them.

Thich Nhat Hahn shared that mindfulness is a way of being rather than something one does. He said " mindfulness is to be aware of what is going on" (Hanh, 2007). In his teachings, he does not promote the idea that mindfulness will somehow eradicate our emotions, but it changes our relationship to our emotions with this offering:

> When you are angry, and if you know that you are angry, that's mindfulness of anger. Mindfulness of anger puts you in a safer position. If you are angry, and if you are not mindful that you are angry, the situation is more dangerous. So, mindfulness of sadness, mindfulness of joy, mindfulness of anger, mindfulness of drinking, mindfulness of walking, mindfulness of breathing, mindfulness of cooking; mindfulness can be practiced at every moment of your daily life. And by that, you cultivate the energy of mindfulness.

I have watched educators teach mindfulness with an intense emphasis on slowness. However, if we use Thich Nhat Hanh's approach to mindfulness, we can be moving quickly and, as long as we are aware of this quickness, we are engaging in mindfulness.

Mindfulness in our overly busy society can seem like an impossible practice. Yet, I believe we are in desperate need of people who are moving with more awareness, rather than less. We need practices that help us to recognize and make sense of our inner experiences and the world around us. We also need to engage in these practices with others so that we are continuously expanding our understanding of our world through the stories, perceptions, and realities of other people.

There are various teachings connected to mindfulness that center *acceptance*. I want to emphasize that *acceptance* should not be thought of as being synonymous with *complacency*. Acceptance means that we are recognizing the truth of a moment and reality as it is, not as we wish it to be. From that place of acceptance, we can make intentional choices to interrupt and disrupt beliefs, patterns, and practices that are harmful to ourselves, each other, and the broader world. It's not a "Oh well, that's just the way things are" mentality. Rather, it is a framing of "This is the way things are. The way things are is causing harm. I would like to be part of the change that alleviates the harm and suffering." Exploring and examining your upbringing and experiences in childhood, including your social identities/social group memberships, can help us to uncover some of our woundedness (Kirk & Okazawa-Rey, 2018; Tatum, 2018). This is not always a comfortable process and may drudge up some wounds we thought had healed.

Chapter 1 will provide a very brief introduction to mindfulness and I will introduce some foundational mindfulness practices. In Chapter 2, I will introduce applied and relational mindfulness practices. In the second part, we will build more self-awareness. In Chapter 3, we will begin to explore our emotional landscapes, the origins of our relationship with our emotions, with a particular focus on shame, guilt, and shame avoidance. Chapter 4 will provide an introduction to socialization and social identities. In Chapter 5, we will explore our values and beliefs and Chapter 6 will give insight into the experiences of burnout.

Chapters 7 through 10 will provide information about power and uses of power within schools and school systems. Chapter 7 will examine power in schools and Chapter 8 will identify where bias is permeating our schools. Chapter 9 will connect biases to social identities and Chapter 10 will problematize control in our schools.

Chapters 11 through 14. will support you in finding ways to build and develop school and school system cultures organized around collaborative change work (Chapter 11), engaging in generative conflict (Chapter 12), and relational repair (Chapter 13). The concluding chapter will invite you to reflect on your power within the system and how you want to engage in ongoing change work.

Additionally, you will find affirmations at the ends of Chapters 4–13 to support you in your journey of learning and unlearning.

This work doesn't have an end. There is no destination point we will arrive at that will indicate we have no more learning, unlearning, or change to do. That is not the goal. The goal is to stay fiercely loving in our resolve to care for ourselves and others in a way that is centered around disrupting conditions that create harm and co-creating conditions that offer room for healing and wholeness.

1

Mindfulness

Learning to Be in the Moment

The Magic of Mindfulness

Since the 1970s, mindfulness and mindfulness-based practices have increased in popularity in the U.S. (Hanh, 2007; Purser, 2019). People buy apps, books, retreats, curricula, card decks, calendars, and journals in pursuit of building more mindfulness into their days and lives. Sometimes the habits stick, and other times these practices get lost when we get bogged down into the chaos of the news, the unsustainable pace of the school day and school year, and our everyday lives.

Many studies highlight the beneficial aspects of mindfulness-based practices for educators. These practices can reduce stress and increase job satisfaction (Akhavan et al., 2021; Hülsheger et al., 2013; Matiz et al., 2025). This is also true for educators actively engaged in social justice and activism (Gorski, 2015). There are many different forms of mindfulness practices, which include breathing, listening, and walking. They also include practices like reflective journaling, loving-kindness, and gratitude practices.

Mindfulness can help us to recognize what is happening for us in any given moment and can help us to understand ourselves

DOI: 10.4324/9781003540687-2

better. In a world filled with busy-ness and technology, we may forget to really tune in to how we are feeling and how our nervous systems are operating. These practices can support our capacity to truly tune into our emotional world.

Mindfulness in Healing and Justice Work

Many mindfulness and mindfulness-based practices practiced in Western cultures have been adapted from Buddhist practices within collectivist cultures. Mindfulness taken out of its roots from collectivist cultures and promoted as a self-improvement practice can have unintended consequences. There is no benefit to engaging in some kind of competition to see who can be "more mindful" nor should there be a sense of moral superiority if we practice mindfulness while others around us do not.

In fact, using mindfulness as a self-improvement practice can increase selfishness and self-centeredness especially in people who have been raised within hyper-individualistic cultures (Kucinskas, 2019; Poulin et al., 2021; Purser, 2019). If we approach our mindfulness practice as a solo project, then we miss out on expanding our understanding of our world through awareness of ourselves in the world as complex people, expanding our awareness of others, and the connection between ourselves and other people and the broader world.

Mindfulness practices are not cure-alls and will not resolve the many external sources of your stressors. These practices can support our capacity for comfort with the healthy discomfort that comes from becoming more aware of injustices in our schools, and in the world more broadly. They will not, and should not, lead us to caring less about issues of justice in our schools and in the world. The intention of these practices is to give you the time and space to truly be present and to tend to your inner world so that you have the capacity to do the beautiful and important work you do each day.

Cumulative Stress and Overwhelm

Dr. Rochelle Arms Almengor, in *Colorizing Restorative Justice: Voicing Our Realities* (2020), wrote:

> schools are microcosms of the greater society; they concentrate the strengths and ills of their members' communities. This social concentration means that racism, violence, and other challenges to mental and emotional well-being are felt more intensely within the pressure cooker of a school environment, where almost everything occurs in plain view.

This is the reality of working in schools. Mindfulness practices will not eradicate this reality, but they can support us in recognizing the impact being in this "pressure cooker" environment has on our own nervous systems and the nervous systems of everyone connected to schools including families and students.

The pace of the school day and the entire school year is frustratingly fast. The constant urgency creates tension in the system and tension in the people in the system. The pressure placed upon educators by people within and outside the school system to maximize learning by pushing students through content or a literacy program negatively impacts educators, students, families, and even administrators. No one is well in an environment focused on performance and perfectionism. Using mindfulness-based practices can support us in slowing down enough to be aware of our emotional landscape and can alleviate stress and overwhelm.

There are many images of people looking peaceful and serene when practicing mindfulness, whether it is meditation or yoga. The truth is that sitting in stillness and quiet can be incredibly uncomfortable if we are not used to it. Being with our thoughts, emotions, and sensations without any distractions can feel overwhelming. As we develop the capacity to be with those experiences of overwhelm, it can be helpful to have some words to wrap around our inner worlds. We will start by expanding our language of emotions and language of sensations.

Building Our Emotional Vocabulary

No emotions are bad. I'm going to write that again. No emotions are bad. There are many ways to understand our emotional landscapes and there are schools of thought that categorize emotions as "negative" or "positive." We may experience emotions that feel uncomfortable. Part of this discomfort may be because of the cultural and familial messaging we received in our youth. Our experiences of emotions are highly dependent on our socialization and cultural messaging (Barrett, 2017). This concept will be addressed in more detail in Chapter 3. For now, to support your building of mindfulness practices, we will explore emotional granularity and a tool that can help us build our emotional vocabulary.

Emotional Granularity

In workshops, I often ask people to share with a partner how they are feeling. Many people respond with statements like "I'm feeling pretty good" or "Yeah, I'm fine today" or "Huh, I haven't really thought about it...but I mean I'm here so I guess I'm alright." None of those statements contain an emotion. This ability to identify our emotions with a high level of accuracy and acuity is called *emotional granularity,* a term coined by Dr. Lisa Feldman Barrett (Barrett, 2004; Barrett et al., 2001).

One of my favorite tools for building emotional granularity is a feelings wheel. This tool was originally designed by Gloria Willcox in 1982 in her article entitled *The Feeling Wheel: A tool for expanding awareness of emotions and increasing spontaneity and intimacy*. Below is an adaptation of a feeling wheel using the original feeling wheel and Dr. Albert Wong's feeling wheel (2023). The italicized headings in the chart are more coarse emotions that are often easier to identify. The emotions below each header are related to the headers but are more specific.

numb	*scared*	*mad*	*powerful*	*happy*
checked out	small	annoyed	courageous	elated
flat	inferior	frustrated	hopeful	pleased
bored	humiliated	angry	confident	joyful
disinterested	vulnerable	furious	proud	delighted
absent	frightened	irritated	assured	playful

numb	*scared*	*mad*	*powerful*	*happy*
apathetic	nervous	indignant	satisfied	energized
stuck	anxious	hostile	important	connected
	overwhelmed	rageful	respected	interested
	lost	critical	encouraged	engaged
	afraid	bitter		eager
	frightened	grandiose		
	alone	belligerent		
sad	*disgust*	*stress*	*surprise*	*peaceful*
disappointed	disdain	overwhelmed	bewildered	calm
let down	disapproval	busy	amazed	nurturing
lonely	revulsion	chaotic	shocked	caring
dejected	shock	flustered	excited	grateful
hurt	horror	puzzled	astonished	trusting
fragile	aversion	confused	fascinated	relaxed
grief	nauseous	pressure	curious	thoughtful
despair	judgy	tense	confused	content
despondent	squeamish	incompetent		tender
longing	unpleasant			gentle
remorseful				loving
heartbroken				warm

People with high levels of emotional granularity experience less distress with high-intensity emotions, including depression and anxiety. Conversely, people with lower levels of emotional granularity may feel these emotions more intensely and feel them longer (Barrett et al. 2001; Kashdan et al. 2015; Smidt and Suvak 2015; Tan et al. 2022; Wilson-Mendenhall and Dunne 2021). Because emotions are embodied - experienced by our bodies in addition to our minds - when building our emotional landscape vocabulary, it can be helpful to have words to describe physical sensations. The chart below offers a variety of words that can jumpstart your sensation vocabulary expansion.

soft	floppy	constricted	active	distinct
rigid	steely	fluid	sluggish	shapeless
tense	loud	sluggish	expansive	slimy

relaxed	quiet	vibrant	constricted	arid
spacious	achy	bright	delicate	strong
dense	easeful	dull	strong	weak
jumbled	empty	sticky	immense	tender
clear	full	consistent	miniscule	firm
tingly	jagged	tinny	crumbly	woozy
sharp	smooth	sonorous	solid	steady

Mindfulness practices invite us to be in the moment and to learn how to navigate our emotional and sensory states with curiousness and openness. Both our ability to name our emotions and our capacity to be with uncomfortable emotional experiences are skills we can learn, not innate or fixed traits. Everyone has the capacity to increase their ability to more accurately identify their own emotions.

Mindfulness-Based Practices to Explore

Many people may think of mindfulness as sitting still and clearing the mind. This is a form of mindfulness, but does not necessarily have to be the mindfulness practice you start exploring. If we force ourselves to be completely still when our body, mind, and/or heart are not ready for that level of hyper-awareness, it can feel very overwhelming. Mindfulness-based practices that focus on stillness and calmness can feel very overwhelming for some people.

Sitting in quiet can intensify the awareness of overwhelm and it may bring up memories that we have stored away. There are many reasons that people will dislike various practices, and even seemingly simple practices, like guided breathing, can unintentionally cause distress for some people. This was true for me very early on in my practice. Trying to control my breath in any way would cause me to feel panicked and I would feel intensely anxious. It took me many years of practice, trying different techniques with a variety of teachers, to find breathing practices that felt relaxing instead of distressing. One of my yoga teachers suggested we should not teach anything we haven't practiced at least 10,000 times. That humbled me and reminded me of the importance of building my own mindfulness practice before trying to teach them to others.

Learning how to be still and to be with our thoughts, emotions, and physical sensations can be very uncomfortable for some of us. For other people, it may feel completely easeful and natural. Neither experience is better than the other; they are just simply experiences. These practices will be experienced differently by different people at different times. We should never mandate mindfulness nor force anyone to practice guided mindfulness practices, nor can it be assumed that people will find them relaxing.

These practices should not be used to anesthetize ourselves or pressure ourselves to be in a calm state all the time. Mindfulness practices can support our nervous systems in finding a state of calm, but the goal should not be to make oneself or someone else calm. These practices can and are weaponized, and they should never be used as tools of compliance, emotional suppression, and control.

Additionally, mindfulness practices should not be used solely when you or someone else is in an agitated or collapsed nervous system state. Never in history has anyone ever "calmed down" because someone said they should. That message often has an immediate rejection response and will likely increase someone's agitation. Mindfulness should be practiced many, many times in a relatively calm and relaxed state long before trying to use them when our nervous systems are flooded. Our bodies and minds will then associate these practices with a sense of calm and ease and not with a sense of being scolded.

When our nervous systems are overloaded, and we begin to introduce mindfulness, the practices may feel agitating or like they "aren't working." A mindfulness teacher once explained that if we feel tired during a mindfulness practice, the practice isn't making us tired. Rather, we have slowed down enough to recognize that we are, in fact, tired. Far too often, especially in schools, we are in a perpetual state of alertness and/or exhaustion which is no good for anyone or for the work we do. Mindfulness practices can support our nervous systems in moving into a state of rest and digest. This state is important as we embark on change work within ourselves and within the systems we are working in.

There is no need to try many different practices. Sometimes, simple is best. Repetition also helps support us in reflecting on our inner worlds and how we respond to the practices. It can also take time for a practice to start to feel relaxing and beneficial when our nervous systems interpret this change as a threat. This is a very normal experience for people when trying on new practices, especially ones that are practiced in quiet and stillness. Let's explore some foundational mindfulness practices that can create room for us to recognize our emotional states and the state of our nervous system. These practices are to both build awareness and to learn how to soothe and relax our nervous systems.

Tuning-In Practices

These practices can be done by yourself in a quiet enough space or with others. If you are using these in a group, these tuning-in practices are akin to parallel play; you are engaging in the same activity near others, but you aren't conversing with others.

These practices build your capacity to be in touch with your experience and to be in the present moment. This is simple, but it is not always easy. Our minds will wander, and we will get distracted by a thought, or a sound, or something we see. Each time you notice your mind wandering, gently invite yourself to return to the practice. You will get to know your inner critic quite well in these moments.

Our inner critics might sound like "See, you did it again. You're always distracted" or "What is wrong with me? Why can't I just focus for like two seconds?" That inner critic is trying to help us get back on track, but that hint of shaming will not actually support us in changing habits. It might even lead us to give up or believe we just can't practice mindfulness. Rather than trying to push that inner critic as far away as possible or meeting it with a different inner critic "listen, I'm trying to be mindful, can you just go away?!", build in gentle redirections.

A gentler redirection might sound like any of these: "It's true I got distracted. That's normal," "Huh, it seems it's very busy in my mind today," or "Oops, I wandered off again." Then just return to your practice. In the words of Terry Real (2022), a relationship therapist: "there is nothing that harshness does that loving firmness doesn't do better" (p. 9). Being gentle with ourselves makes a world of difference as we build our capacity for change.

In the next pages are foundational practices that we can use to build our ability to be fully present in the moment. These practices can be done anywhere. It can be helpful to start them in a relatively quiet space. If you don't have access to such an area, you will still benefit from these practices. Rather than a perfectly quiet place, you can find a place that is relatively distraction-reduced. This might be challenging for any number of reasons. Finding the time in your busy day may also be challenging. You could try replacing 5 minutes of internet/social media zone out time with these practices.

The practices below are ordered intentionally for exploration. However, you do not need to follow them in any particular order. You can randomly pick one or two to start with, or you can choose the ones you think will work best for you. I recommend starting with one or two practices and trying them at least 3-5 times for a couple of weeks. You can also use the guided audio recordings available online or record yourself while exploring these practices.

As you explore these, it can be helpful to set an intention to be curious rather than analytical. This curious mindset is easier said than done, but it becomes easier with practice. It may also be helpful to label experiences as *pleasant*, *unpleasant*, or *neutral*. Those broad categories can help you stay tuned in and aware of your experience without going into the story of *why*. If one of these practices starts to create a high level of discomfort and overwhelm, or even a sense of panic, you do not have to force yourself to continue the practice.

Mindful Walking

We move around our physical world all the time. We are often moving without awareness of how we move and what the experience of moving is like. Start with 5 or 10 minutes for this practice. This can be done inside or outside, at your workplace/school or at home. It may be less distracting to walk somewhere outside, of your home if you, like me, get distracted by dishes that need to be done or the dust you realized accumulated on the TV or the stack of ungraded papers on your desk.

If you use assistive devices or a wheelchair, adjust the language here so it makes sense for your experience. The most important part is feeling your body connected to the Earth below you whether you are moving on feet, wheels, or feet and an assistive device.

Before starting the practice, set an intention to focus on the sensations and experience of moving across the ground/the Earth. Remind yourself to find a gentle internal nudge to return to the experience each time your mind wanders. Take written or mental notes of how you feel before you start; use the feelings chart and/or the sensations chart.

If it is helpful, you can set a timer for 5 or 10 minutes. You can always extend the practice as time allows. Start with a comfortable pace. Notice what happens as you increase your awareness of *how* you are moving and what it feels like. You may find that it feels easier to focus on your experience by moving at a slightly slower pace. It might feel awkward and you may be hyperaware of your movement patterns. That is completely normal and the self-consciousness will eventually fade. Labeling sensations or experiences as *pleasant, unpleasant*, or *neutral* might be helpful. After the timer goes off, take a moment to reflect on how you feel now compared to the start of the practice.

Awareness of Sounds

For this practice, you can have your eyes opened or closed. There are times when closing our eyes can create more internal overwhelm. That's normal and happens to many people. You can stand, sit, or lie down. If you are keeping your eyes open, find a neutral place to focus your gaze. Preferably not a laundry pile or a stack of mail or a particularly messy desk or a mess of crumbs left behind after snack. You can look out a window or at a spot on the ground, the wall, or the ceiling.

Before you start the practice, set your intention to become more aware of the sounds in your environment. Remind yourself to find a gentle internal nudge to return to the experience each time your mind wanders. Take note of how you feel before you start. Set a timer for your chosen amount of time.

Let your body relax and tune in to the sounds in your environment. As you notice sounds, you might notice that you start to tell a story about the sound. "I wonder if that's my neighbor coming home from work. They're always so noisy" or "Those kids are always stomping around when they come back from lunch." Let those thoughts drift away and instead become aware of the qualities of the sounds. Sharp. Tinny. Constant. Brief. Loud. Quiet. Pitchy. Bassy. Notice if you feel any of the vibrations of the sounds. Notice the ways your body responds and reacts to different sounds. Move toward experiencing the sounds themselves, rather than the stories about the sounds. Try using the labels *pleasant, unpleasant,* and *neutral* as you notice your inner experience of sounds. When the timer goes off, notice the sound of the timer and how your body responds this sound. Then take note of how you feel after closing the practice. You can use the feelings chart and/or the sensations chart.

Colors, Shapes, Textures

For this practice, you can be sitting, lying down, or standing. You can even practice this while moving around a space. If movement becomes too distracting, you can practice this in stillness. You can also explore the differences of your experiences of this practice while moving compared to when practicing in stillness.

Before you start the practice, set your intention to become aware of colors, shapes, and textures in your space. Remind yourself to find a gentle internal nudge to return to the experience each time your mind wanders. Take note of how you feel before you start. Set a timer for your chosen amount of time. I recommend starting with 1-3 minutes for this practice.

From whichever position you are in, slowly move your head to the left. Scan your environment slowly with your eyes. Notice the different colors, shapes, and textures in the space you are in. Notice any colors, shapes, or textures that you particularly like or feel comforting to you. Conversely, notice if there are any that you dislike. Then slowly move your head back to center while taking in more or the same colors, shapes, and textures. Pause and take a breath. Then repeat this by moving your head to the right and back to center. Take note of how you feel after this practice with the feelings chart and/or sensations chart.

Daily Chores

In many of his books and his teachings, Thich Nhat Hanh describes being mindful of what we are doing while we are doing it. That is the true essence of being mindful. He describes practices such as washing the dishes or making a cup of tea. For many of us, these are things we do without awareness. We may be multitasking out of necessity (getting other people in your household ready for their days) or out of habit (listening to a podcast while washing the dishes or making tea).

You can use these practices at your workplace/school or at home. It is up to you to decide which environment will be more easily accessible to practice. Choose something you do daily that you would like to practice doing mindfully. This can be anything like folding laundry, making tea or coffee, washing dishes, or sweeping. Grading or writing emails can be done mindfully and with mindful awareness, but they are often more cognitively and emotionally charged. As you build your practice, start by choosing something that doesn't require a lot of cognitive effort. Before you start, notice how you feel and take note of your thoughts. Set an intention to be fully present to the experience of the task you are doing. Notice sensations on your hands and skin. Notice the movements your body makes. Notice the pace of your movements. Take note of sounds and scents. Try adding the labels *pleasant*, *unpleasant*, and *neutral*.

After completing the task (or part of the task if you didn't have time to tackle the entire chore), take note of how you feel now and what your experience was like with the feelings chart and/or sensations chart.

Awareness of Breath

Breathing is something we do unconsciously in order to stay alive and requires no conscious thought. Some people find sitting in stillness and focusing on their breath to be incredibly anxiety-inducing. Other people find it very calming. For people who have had panic attacks or have a history of breathing challenges, breathwork of any kind can create a strong physiological reaction. This doesn't mean breathwork should be avoided, but it should be practiced with care. It may also be helpful to practice with someone skilled in somatic awareness who can be an anchor for your nervous system as you explore breathwork.

Try this practice sitting, standing, or lying down. You may want to start with lying down with some cushions or pillows while wearing something comfortable. Your eyes can be closed or open. If you are keeping your eyes open, try to focus on one point. Set your intention to be curious about and open to whatever your experience is. You can experiment with labeling sensations as *pleasant, unpleasant,* and *neutral.* Set a timer for your chosen amount of time. It can be helpful to start small and then gradually increase your practice time as your comfort increases. Take note of how you feel before you begin.

For this particular breathing practice, there is no need to try to control the flow or increase the length of your inhales or the exhales. Simply bring awareness to the breath. There are many places our awareness can go when we focus on the breath. The air meeting our nostrils. The sensation of air just below the nostrils. The movement of the in and out breath in the chest or the abdomen. The whole path of the breath on the inhale from the nose, through the throat, the chest, into the abdomen and the out breath moving back up through the abdomen, the chest, the throat, and through the nose. What do you notice about your own breath at this moment?

After the timer, take one more inhale and exhale, and then move your body slowly. Then take note of your experience and how you feel now after the practice with the feelings chart and/or sensations chart.

Physical Sensations/Body Scan

I rarely start with a body scan when introducing mindfulness practices. I also do not do full body scans in professional settings. I only use them when I am teaching yoga and/or if people have consented to the practice beforehand (i.e. signed up for a workshop).

One of the strangest body scans I experienced was guided at work by a cisgender heterosexual man in a room full of mostly cisgender women. He started with bringing awareness to our feet, our legs, skipped over the entire torso, and then went to our arms and head. It was a good move on his part to not ask us to focus our attention on the pelvis or chest for many reasons, but this is exactly why we should not mandate these types of practices or think they are suitable for all settings.

You might not need a timer for this practice. In this practice, lying down is often the most accessible. Being comfortable also helps so that you aren't hyper-focused on feeling too cold, too hot, or like the surface you are on is too hard. You can practice this with your eyes closed or open. Some people find it hard to practice this with their eyes open.

Begin by bringing awareness to your feet. Observe sensations as you bring awareness to the soles of your feet, toes, tops of your feet, ankles, lower legs, knees, then upper legs. Name the qualities of the sensations or label them as *pleasant, unpleasant, or neutral.* Continue moving up through the buttocks, pelvis, hips, abdomen, low back, mid back, upper back, chest. Bring awareness to the fingers and thumbs, backs of the hands, palms of the hands, through the wrists, lower arms, elbows, upper arms, and shoulders. Name the qualities of the sensations or label them as *pleasant, unpleasant, or neutral.* Then move awareness to the throat, the back of the neck, the chin, the jawline, the mouth, cheeks, nose, eyes, brow line, forehead, the ears, then the scalp. Then notice your whole body from the soles of your feet to the top of your head and the constellation of sensations present. Once you have completed the practice, gently move your fingers and toes and then slowly change positions. Then take note of how you feel. Use the feelings chart and/or the sensations chart if it is helpful.

Releasing Tension: An Alternative to a Body Scan

I love this practice as an alternative to a full body scan. It helps bring awareness to our body without overfocusing on any part. You can sit, stand, or lie down for this one. A timer for anywhere between 3 and 10 minutes is a great place to start.

The intention of this practice is to become aware of tension you are holding and to gently release some tension. Some practices and practitioners use the language "release all tension." I do not suggest using this because some of us have chronic tension and it can feel defeating when we aren't able to "release all tension". This practice will not miraculously evaporate tension, but it will help to expand our experience of softening and releasing.

Wherever you are, start by becoming aware of your body and the connections between your body and the surface(s) you are on. Do a brief scan of your body and notice where the most tension is being held. It may be helpful to label the qualities of sensations (sharp, achy, dull, intense, hot, etc.). Don't get too wrapped up in the labels. Then notice your breathing. Notice the quality of your breath (shallow, slow, quick, etc.). Then, with each exhale, invite your body to relax into and across the surface supporting you. Allow yourself to supported by the chair, the couch, the floor, the cushions, or any other surface you are on. Keep releasing into and across that support with each exhale. You may notice that your exhales naturally become longer and slower. When the timer goes off take note of how you feel using the feelings chart and/or the sensations chart. Notice if and how your tension has changed, and how your breath is moving.

Building Your Practice

It can be helpful to choose one or two practices to commit to over a couple of weeks. Blocking the time off in your calendar or putting a sticky note somewhere to remind you to practice can support you in building this new habit. Letting someone else know you are trying this and receiving some social support can also be beneficial. It is not necessary, but it can provide insight to log changes you notice in your practice. Start small, and don't be too hard on yourself if you miss a day.

Just as when our mind wanders during our mindfulness practice, and we offer a gentle invitation to return to the moment, we can be gentle with ourselves as we build our habits of mindfulness. For me that inner talk sometimes sounds like "Hey babe, I know we missed that practice yesterday. It was a particularly rough day, and I just didn't want to sit with my feelings. That's okay. Let's pick up tomorrow." The combination of inner compassion and dedication to follow-through is a potent form of loving accountability. When we don't have the time or bandwidth for the longer practices, we can use mini-practices to reconnect to the present moment throughout the day.

Mini-practices

In the busy-ness of a school day and the responsibilities that we each have after the day is done it can be overwhelming to try to make the time for a formal practice. These mini-practices are short resets that bring us back to the present moment. They also support our nervous systems in moving back toward a more relaxed state during high-stress moments.

Ground and Breath

Take a moment to feel where you are connected to the ground. As you inhale, focus your attention on those connection points and as you exhale, let your body relax into those connection points. Do this one to three times.

Hands and Feet

Move your awareness to your hands and your feet. Wiggle your fingers and toes. Make fists with your hands then release. Scrunch your toes then release. Do this a few times.

Mini Sound Scan

Become aware of three to five different sounds in the room. Silently name the qualities of each sound.

Colors/Shapes

Scan the room. This can be very subtle by just moving your eyes and not rotating your head. Take note of three to five different colors and/or shapes. If one color or shape is one you like, let your gaze stay there for a moment or two.

Exhale

This sounds simple, and it is! We are often unaware that we have been holding our breath. Taking an intentional exhale signals to our nervous systems that we can relax.

CHAPTER SUMMARY

In this chapter, we explored the impact mindfulness can have on our overall well-being. Mindfulness can support us in becoming more aware of our emotional landscape and how we are truly feeling. Mindfulness can support our capacity to navigate the discomfort that can surface when engaging in conversations around justice and injustice in schools/school systems. These practices are not a cure-all; but they are a part of supporting our wellness and building our self-awareness.

2

Applied and Relational Mindfulness Practices

Applied Mindfulness

In the midst of a very busy school day, everyone in the system is juggling so much. An educator who is the only adult in a classroom must pay attention to multiple conversations and monitor the progress and pacing of students during a lesson. An administrator facilitating a staff meeting has to share new information about a budget and hold space for multiple questions while also considering how to respond. Students are navigating complicated social dynamics and trying to meet the expectations of different adults in the school.

Applied mindfulness can be practiced to both navigate stressful or irritating situations and be more present during enjoyable and delightful moments. This form of mindfulness helps us move more smoothly through tough situations and savor the wonderful parts of our days. Practicing applied mindfulness gives us an opportunity to internally slow down.

Applied mindfulness is how we infuse the energy of mindfulness into our daily lives. The particular approach to mindfulness in this book has been influenced by studying with rev. angel Kyodo williams, Thich Nhat Hanh, Lama Rod Owens, and studying their work and the work of many other teachers, in addition to my own personal yoga and meditation practices.

DOI: 10.4324/9781003540687-3

The term "applied mindfulness" originated from the teaching of Thich Nhat Hahn and means that we are using mindfulness throughout our days. He also introduced the phrase "engaged mindfulness," which directly connects mindfulness awareness of social injustices and taking action to disrupt injustices.

We are often rushed during our days and influenced by external pressures to move quickly during the school year. The phrase "We have to get these kids ready" for the next thing, whether it's getting preschoolers ready for kindergarten, or high school students ready for a career path or for college, creates an ever-present sense of urgency. This urgency often prevents us from truly being in any moment. Applied mindfulness is an intentional way of being in each moment with open awareness.

SOAR: Applied Mindfulness

Applied mindfulness is not an easy feat. We should not try to pursue an unrealistic attainment of being fully present all the time. We can, however, build our ability to be more present throughout our days. We can do this with the applied mindfulness practice SOAR: *Soften, Observe, Acknowledge what is, Release judgment*. The elements of SOAR are interconnected and interdependent and do not need to be followed in order; although that can be helpful.

Soften: Softening is essential in bringing ourselves into the present moment. Intentionally softening our body invites our nervous system to move toward a state of relaxation rather than activation. Softening also allows our awareness to expand. It might be helpful to find one part of your body that is the most noticeably tense when you feel stressed or overwhelmed, and practice softening from there.

Observe: Tending to the present moment is essential in any mindfulness practice. Becoming an observer is an intentional focus of this moment and all of its complexities. We observe our inner experience and our surroundings. We can feel the air on our skin, the breath moving through our body, our body in space. We sense our emotions, observe physical sensations, and notice our thoughts. We perceive the people around us and their nonverbal and verbal communications. We take in the physical environment. We hold awareness of ourselves within the space we are in. Softness combined with awareness allows us to have more capacity to take in the complexities and nuances of any given moment.

Acknowledge What Is: When we acknowledge what is, we are recognizing the reality of the moment. When a lesson plan, a meeting, or any other part of the day doesn't play out the way we anticipated, we are likely to get stuck in our thoughts, and we might try to gain control or exert force so things go the way we planned. Rarely does this help us or the people we are with. If we can stay open to what is happening and allow it to unfold without a tight grip of control, then we are more able to be responsive to the moment, rather than trying to control the moment or other people.

Some mindfulness teachers use the term *acceptance* rather than *acknowledge what is*. This shift from *accept* to *acknowledge* is an invitation to be present with what is happening in any given moment while knowing that we do not need to passively accept something that is hurting or harming us or someone else.

Release Judgment: Some people use signs and/or agreements that state "judgment-free zone." I admire the hopefulness that a space with people will be free of judgment. I have never been in such a place. Rather than aspiring to have a "judgment-free zone", we can commit to being aware of and responsible for our judgments. This shift acknowledges and normalizes the reality that we all make judgments and that we can be intentional about addressing them. Releasing judgment supports us in seeing a situation and a person/people as more complex than judgment allows for. For example, if someone is running late to a meeting and our thought is "they are so irresponsible." If we release that judgment it opens up other possibilities: "I wonder why they're late." We may even notice they seem frazzled or stressed. Our perspective becomes curious rather than critical.

In order to change something we must first acknowledge that it is present. When you recognize a judgment you are having, simply name it: "Oh, I'm making a judgment." Then return to the moment. It is completely normal to judge your judgments. "Oh, I'm making a judgment. Why am I doing that? I thought

I was better than that. Ugh. What is wrong with me?!" Totally normal. Notice that and label it: "Oh I'm judging myself for my judgements." Then let it go. You may start to become aware of the types of judgments you have. The chapter on social biases will help you explore this more.

Practicing SOAR

Accessing SOAR in real time will take time, practice, and a lot of feeling awkward and like you're "not getting it." If these practices are completely new to you, I strongly encourage you to practice these in very low-stress environments before trying them in higher-stress situations (like meetings or the busiest time in your work with students). For people who struggle with perfectionism (myself included), it can feel very frustrating to not "get it" or be able to "just do the thing" easily at first. I encourage you to think back to something you learned as an adult that you are now skilled at, like improv, knitting, rock climbing, calligraphy, and remember the very early days of when you were learning. There were likely some very humbling moments along your learning journey. The reason you are skilled now is because you learned through the mistakes, missteps, and found joy in the moments when something clicked. This is no different.

Depending on how much time you have, pick a favorite short TV show episode, song, or some other piece of art that you enjoy. Practice the elements of SOAR. After you finish this, write down or voice record what you noticed. The next time you practice, choose another episode, song, or another piece of art. Choose something that isn't your favorite, but isn't something you detest. Find something you feel neutral about. Practice the elements of SOAR: *Soften, Observe, Acknowledge what is, Release judgment.* After you finish this, write down or voice-record what you noticed. For the next practice, choose an episode, song, or piece of art that you strongly dislike. Practice the elements of SOAR. After you finish this, write down or voice-record what you noticed.

Once you start feeling comfortable with each of the elements and noticing how they work for you in *pleasant, unpleasant,* and *neutral* experiences, start bringing this into your classroom, your work with students, conversations with caregivers, and meetings. Another practice that can support us in truly being in a moment is *deep listening*.

Deep Listening

Many of us have been taught to look the part of being good listeners. In my role as a speech language pathologist, and in observations in classrooms and schools there is often an unhelpful overemphasis on requiring students to "make eye contact with the speaker." Students were encouraged to turn their bodies toward the person talking to show they were listening. Eye contact can be overwhelming for neurodivergent people and is not always culturally appropriate. Looking at someone's face and having your body turned toward someone does not mean you are listening; it just means you are acting like a listener. I can be acting like a listener and be completely tuning you out. There is more on this in the appendix; feel free to skip to that part before moving on. So, how do we practice deep listening?

In an interview in 2010, Thich Nhat Hahn described deep listening as a practice "to relieve the suffering in us, and in the other person. That kind of listening is described as compassionate listening. You listen only for the purpose of relieving suffering in the other person" (n.p). Deep listening can be very challenging during the hectic pace of a school day and when our emotions or someone else's emotions are running high. However, the impact of not practicing deep listening causes much distress and miscommunication. We miss a lot when we are partially listening and making assumptions about what someone is saying or what someone needs from us.

In deep listening, we are not trying to find solutions or problem-solve for someone else. We are simply holding space and bearing witness to someone else. In a 2019 workshop, rev. angel Kyodo williams taught a specific listening practice called "tracking." In this practice, the listener silently repeats what they hear the person say. That's it. It is incredibly simple but can be incredibly challenging. Some people find that they naturally listen this way. For others, it can feel completely overwhelming. Your only focus is their words. When we practice tracking, we notice just how often our mind wanders or how quickly we jump into problem-solving mode.

While you build this practice, you will begin to become very familiar with how you listen to people. People often share that they will paraphrase or try to memorize everything someone is saying. However, when we create paraphrasing shortcuts we are filtering someone else's words and story through our way of using words. In this listening practice, it is critical to really work toward being in another person's story. This helps us to fully understand them without our filtration system or interpretation. This is particularly important when we are listening to people with whom we do not share social identities. Deep listening supports our capacity for empathy to believe the experiences of people with whom we do not share lived experiences. There will be more on empathy in Chapters 9 and 13.

As with all mindfulness-based practices, it is essential that we start building in these practices when we are relatively at ease. I don't suggest trying to practice tracking at the end of a long day or when you are feeling particularly stressed. I also suggest first trying this practice with someone with whom you have a good relationship. Practice with someone with whom your nervous system feels relatively settled and relaxed. It can be helpful to embody SOAR: *Soften, Observe, Acknowledge what is, and Release judgment.*

You can try this on the phone, during a video call, or in-person. Notice the difference between in-person compared to other types of listening settings. I recommend letting your conversation partner know that you are practicing deep listening. It can feel a little odd for people if you are not responding in your usual way.

This practice doesn't necessarily replace other listening practices either. The listening strategies people often reference are more about how you respond and not about *how* you are listening, such as reflective listening. With reflective listening, the intention is to relay someone's message to you back to them. You can still practice tracking in the context of reflective listening. It may even shift your responses.

I do not suggest that you always practice tracking. There are times when we are simply too fatigued to drop into deep listening. It is perfectly okay to let someone know that you do not have the capacity to listen with your whole self at the moment. It might feel like you are being unkind, but it is kinder to yourself and to the person sharing a story that you cannot give them your undivided attention. For people with whom you have close relationships with, you can try phrases like "I want to be fully present to what you are sharing, but I am distracted right now. Can we reconnect tomorrow?" or "I know this is so important, and right now I'm not in a space to be a great listener". Find words that are authentic to you and that are supportive of you, the other person, and your relationship. It is also important to remember that there is no obligation that you are in this type of close relationship with everyone. Your phrasing will also be different when talking with youth. We will continue to explore boundaries throughout the book.

Contemplative Reflection

Some practitioners and researchers combine mindfulness and contemplative practices, others separate them, and there is no universal agreed-upon delineation between these practices. We may need to gain some perspective, understand our own or someone else's emotional response, or puzzle out a complex situation. Contemplative practices give us the opportunity to do exactly that.

As noted in the introduction, throughout this book, there will be reflection questions embedded into the chapters. There will be suggestions on timing. It may be helpful to have one place to keep your notes while you move through this book as all of the questions are interconnected. Before each reflection, it may be helpful to practice one of the mindfulness practices, mini-practices, or any other form of grounding/centering practice that supports you in moving into a more relaxed and open state. The questions are not part of a quiz or a test; they were created to support your analysis of what is happening for you and within your school system and broader community.

In a 2019 talk for a cohort in the Transformative Educational Leadership (TEL) program, Curtiss Sarikey, Chief of Oakland Staff, shared this wisdom:

> Our larger cultures and institutions are all about goals; we value people to get shit done; there's this thing about just do do do. Do more, do it faster, and do it better. And that focus on just the act and not the quality actually replicates the same behaviors, actions that continue to maintain the status quo in our institutions and our communities when we actually want to see change. Systems change, changing the actual environments in which inequities and injustice lives can only happen through a fundamental shift in the quality of our leadership and in our actual being.
>
> *(n.p.)*

Practicing mindfulness and using contemplative reflection to slow down and be thoughtful rather than fast is how we can support our nervous systems in staying steadier through change work. I encourage you to slow down, settle in, and even put the pen down or keyboard away before you start replying. Really take the time to consider the questions rather than trying to move through them.

Activating and choosing curiosity, wonder, and hope can support us in expanding our perceptions rather than believing we have it all figured out. None of us has it all figured out and we likely never will.

Relational Mindfulness Practices

The foundational and mini-practices in Chapter 1 support us in becoming more aware of ourselves and our environment. We also need practices to remember our connection to other people and the broader world. These include: gratitude practices and loving-kindness practices.

Gratitude

Gratitude practices can be incredibly powerful in reducing stress, anxiousness, overwhelm, and frustration and in increasing pleasant and pleasant emotional experiences like happiness, contentment, and appreciation. (Diniz et al., 2023; Gordon et al., 2012). Using gratitude practices reminds us of the beauty in our world and the incredible people in our lives. Just as with any other mindfulness practice, a gratitude practice should not be used to promote avoidance of reality. Rather, this is to help move us out of our negativity bias for a more balanced perspective of our world and our lives.

At the end of the day, take 5 or so minutes to reflect back on the day. Find at least 5 moments, events, something you witnessed, heard, overheard, or were part of that you are grateful for. It is not required, but it can be helpful to have a designated journal for your practice.

An Alternative Gratitude Practice: Highlight/Low/Hero

This is a wonderful variation of a gratitude practice. There are similar versions such as the rose/bud/thorn practice. There are many variations of this that can be used as a self-reflection or a team reflection. This practice can be shared with youth and with adults in small group or whole group settings.

Take some time to reflect on your day as a whole. As you scroll through your memory, notice if there was one *highlight* that happened in your day. It doesn't need to be anything monumental; it just matters that it felt like a *highlight* for you and brought you happiness, ease, joy, delight, or any other pleasant emotion.

Then bring to mind something that was a *low* in your day. Something that didn't go well or was unpleasant in your day. The most important part of this practice is to reflect on what you learned from this experience. What insight did you gain? What perspective was helpful? What would you do differently next time?

The final part is *hero*. Think about someone who showed up in a way that you admire. Or it could be that someone supported you and helped you during a challenging time. It might be you! You might have done something courageous or perhaps you helped someone.

Loving-Kindness Practices

This is one of my favorite practices. Loving-kindness practices are supportive of decreasing stress responses, increasing compassion and empathy, alleviating psychological distress, and promoting overall wellness (Hofmann et al., 2011; Petrovic et al., 2024; Wong et al., 2022). As with all practices, some people will find this enjoyable while others may experience this as emotionally intense. Your experience is not a problem. If we are actively grieving a recent loss, this may feel particularly challenging and emotionally intense. Our emotional responses are nothing to be ashamed of (more on this in the next chapter). If you are feeling joy, sadness, overwhelm, frustration, or impatience, just notice your experience and allow those emotions to flow.

There are many variations of this practice that you can find online and in texts. You are also welcome to modify or change the words to suit you and your practice. We start by wishing wellness for/to ourselves. Then to someone we know well and care about. We then send these well-wishes to someone we don't know well but might see regularly. Then we send these wishes out to a broader community and to the whole world.

It may be helpful to record this practice or ask someone whose voice you find soothing to make a recording for you. You can also access the audio recordings made for readers of this book available online. You can use this practice anywhere you would like as long as you can feel relatively able to focus without distractions or interruptions. This can be done sitting, standing, lying down, or even on your commute on public transportation. I don't suggest using this while you are driving. Your eyes can be closed or you can hold your gaze somewhere neutral. This practice is easier to do with your eyes closed because it involves accessing your imagination. Some people enjoy placing one or both hands on their heart while doing this practice.

Take a moment to get comfortable and to soften your shoulders, jaw, and abdomen. We will start by wishing wellness to ourselves. As you repeat these wishes silently to yourself, imagine yourself embodying these qualities. You can also imagine someone who cares for you deeply sending these wishes to you if it feels challenging to wish yourself well.

May I feel safe | I wish myself safety.
May I feel protected | I wish myself protection.
May I feel healthy | I wish myself health.
May I feel at ease | I wish for myself to feel at ease.

Take a moment to feel these well-wishes being sent from yourself to yourself. Now, bring someone to mind that you care deeply about. As you imagine them, send them wishes of wellness.

May you feel safe | I wish you safety.
May you feel protected | I wish you protection.
May you feel healthy | I wish you health.
May you feel at ease | I wish for you to feel at ease.

Take a moment to notice how you feel sending these wishes of wellness to someone you are deeply about. Bring someone to mind who you may not know well. Someone you do not feel frustration with nor a strong social connection with. As you imagine them, send them wishes of wellness.

May you feel safe | I wish you safety.
May you feel protected | I wish you protection.
May you feel healthy | I wish you health.
May you feel at ease | I wish for you to feel at ease.

Take a moment and notice how you feel after sending these wishes of wellness to this person. Now, expand your awareness to people you know and love and people you don't know or don't feel strongly connected to. You can imagine your block, your street, then imagine the whole town or city, then the state, the country, and the whole world and all beings including plants, and animals.

May we all feel safe | I wish us all safety.
May we all feel protected | I wish us all protection.
May we all feel healthy | I wish us all health.
May we all feel at ease | I wish for us all to feel at ease.

Pause and notice how you feel after sending these well-wishes out as far as your imagination could stretch. If your eyes have been closed, slowly open them and take in your surroundings. Move and gently stretch your body in any way that you need.

Note: *I encourage you to wait until the last chapter about teaching mindfulness to others before introducing this one in particular to youth. This one can be introduced to adults with less caution but do read the last chapter before teaching this to others.*

CHAPTER SUMMARY

Applied mindfulness practices allow for us to be in the present moment. SOAR, *soften, observe, acknowledge what is,* and *release judgment,* is a practice we can use throughout our days and can be particularly useful in stressful situations. Deep listening is a practice of tuning into someone else's story without overlaying our own thoughts, opinions, or giving advice. These practices support us in receiving the moment as it is rather than reacting to it. Approaching contemplative reflection with curiosity, wonder, and hope can support us in truly considering what is happening for us and our setting with. We also need practices to remind us of our connection to other people and the broader world.

3

Beginning to Explore Our Emotional Landscape

We are emotional beings, and emotions are complex. Emotions contain both thoughts and physical sensations, and they influence our behavior. Our relationship to our emotional landscape is incredibly complex. In Chapter 1, we briefly explored the importance and power of *emotional granularity* (Barrett et al., 2001): the ability to precisely label our emotional experience. Emotional granularity can be practiced and learned. Developing and honing our skills of emotional granularity promotes our overall well-being and supports us in being responsive to our emotional needs.

The Origins of Our Relationship with Emotions

Our current ability to recognize and label our emotions and our capacity to navigate our emotions, is directly connected to our upbringing, including the cultural expectations around emotional expression. All of these factors directly influence our relationship to not only our own emotions, but to the emotions of others. Our upbringings taught us which emotions are socially acceptable to express and which were deemed socially unacceptable. If we were raised to be expressive with our anger and frustration, we may be very comfortable when other people express

DOI: 10.4324/9781003540687-4

their anger and frustration with raised voices and emphatic gestures. Conversely, if we were raised to believe anger is something to avoid and is dangerous, we likely suppress our own anger and may feel very uncomfortable when people express their frustrations.

If we were raised in a way that discouraged us from expressing exuberance, we may stifle joy and feel a tension in our bodies when we start to feel something close to joy. We may also try to clamp down on others when they are expressing exuberant joy. However, if we were raised in a way that celebrated exuberant displays of joy, we are likely to delight in experiencing this and celebrate others when they are expressing this also. If you were discouraged from being sad or showing fear, you may label those emotions as "negative." You may have received lots of praise and a sense of belonging when you were focused and calm, so that you may now label those emotions as "positive." Neither joy nor sadness can be objectively described as either positive or negative; rather, they are emotions that are differently experienced by different people.

Reflecting on Our Upbringing

For this next practice, I invite you to take about twenty minutes or more where you can be undisturbed. For those of you caring for others in your home, this may be a challenge. If it is more accessible to do this at a library, a coffee shop, or at school or your workplace, do that! You may need to break this activity into a few different sessions.

This reflection may evoke intense emotions and memories. Be gentle with yourself. If these questions begin to feel too overwhelming or bring up memories that are too daunting to face alone, work with a trusted confidant to support your work.

Revisit the feelings chart in Chapter 1 or use any feelings wheel visual that is helpful for you and take some time to reflect. You can do this over the course of a few days, weeks, or even months. In order to truly change our relationships with emotions, we need deep reflection rather than perfunctory task completion. Revisit this practice from time to time as you continue to grow and change.

Reflecting on Our Emotional Socialization:

- In your youth, reflect on places you were socialized (e.g. home, school, religious communities, etc.):
    - What emotions were you encouraged to show?
        - What subtle and overt messages did you receive?
    - What emotions were you discouraged from showing?
        - What subtle and overt messages did you receive?

After finishing this reflection, reread what you wrote. What do you notice? How do you feel? What did you discover or remember? You may find it is helpful to revisit this practice from time to time. You may find it helpful to periodically revisit these prompts as you move through this book and experience different emotions.

Taking the time to reflect on the origins of your relationship to emotions takes courage. Understanding our histories supports us in changing our relationship with emotions in the present.

Reflecting on Our Relationship with Emotions and Sensations

This reflection is intended to help you build more awareness of your current relationship with emotions. In a workshop I facilitated, one participant noted that, after looking through the feelings wheel, they realized they, in fact, do experience these emotions, but that they had spent many years suppressing or avoiding certain emotions. This is true for many people, since our culture is primarily focused on prioritizing logic and rationality over emotionality. There is nothing wrong with you if you don't currently have a high awareness of your emotional states; it just means you haven't had enough opportunities to practice.

For this practice, use your chosen feelings vocabulary tool. There may be words on it that you don't connect with; that's entirely okay. There may also be words on there that you dislike or would use a synonym for; that's also great. You can make your own wheel or emotions chart that can best reflect words in a way that makes sense for you. Do that later, though. Right now, just get familiar with some of these words. If you feel overwhelmed by the sheer number of words, then cover up parts of it, and focus on one section at a time.

For this reflection practice, set aside at least 10 minutes, or more if you can find the time. Reflect on the questions below based on your current relationship with emotions:

- Which emotions create restriction and tension in your body?
- Which emotions bring softness and ease in your body?
- Which emotions are you comfortable feeling or expressing to others?
- Which emotions are you afraid of feeling or expressing to others?
- Which emotions do you try to avoid or suppress?

After completing this reflection, take a moment to move around, stretch, or take a short walk (inside or outside). You could even return to one of the foundational mindfulness practices from Chapter 1. Then, revisit what you wrote, and take note of any patterns or particularly useful information you uncovered and/or remembered.

Name It to Navigate It

A few years ago I posted on Instagram a reframe of "name it to tame it" (Siegel & Bryson, 2012), relabeling it as "name it to navigate it." Our emotions carry so much important information. At times, we may feel that our emotions are going to overwhelm us—and sometimes they do—but we don't need to *tame* our emotions; we need to *understand* them. Through mindfulness, we can become more aware of our emotions and respond to them, rather than try to squash them down or pretend they don't exist.

There are many reasons we suppress our emotions. We may have been discouraged from displaying certain emotions in our youth and we now associate them with being rejected or being told to stop being sad, mad, or too joyful. The culture of the workplace may, implicitly and explicitly, communicate that everyone must get along and be kind. Any conflict or disagreement is met with too many smiles and messages akin to "let's just agree to disagree," while not addressing the conflict at all (more on conflict in Chapter 12). This emotional suppression takes a toll on us emotionally, physically, and socially (Chapman et al., 2013; Quartana & Burns, 2010; Srivastava et al., 2009).

Emotional navigation does not mean we move through the world loudly proclaiming how we feel to everyone all the time. Instead, it means we take a moment to understand the emotion we are experiencing and name it to ourselves. This simple, yet often-challenging, practice reduces stress and gives us more choice in any moment, especially when we are experiencing energetically intense emotions such as fear, anger, frustration, irritation, and overwhelm. The more we can be with our emotions, the more we begin to understand our emotional world, and we build our capacity to make conscious choices about what to do to care for our emotions.

By being with feelings, I do not mean filling up a bathtub with your shame, guilt, fear, anxiousness, and agitation and continuously allowing that to permeate your whole being. Rather, I mean developing a practice in which you can simultaneously observe and witness those emotions and sensations without being stuck in them. It also means not denying the reality that we are emotional beings with emotional responses and emotional needs.

Emotional Avoidance

There may be times when we do not know what we are feeling or why we are experiencing an emotion, particularly emotions that are unpleasant, such as anger, fear, sadness, and overwhelm. Recognizing our habits when our emotions feel like they are "too much" can lead us toward a better way of relating to and moving out of these emotions that might feel "stuck."

However, emotional avoidance is not always a problem; instead, it can be viewed as a self-protection strategy. At times, we might need to not fully feel an emotion. In moments of intense conflict, if someone is belittling us or continuously talking over us, it might not be possible to fully embrace and process our emotions. Recognizing when we need to press pause in a conversation or remove ourselves from a situation is also a part of skillfully navigating our emotions. Learning our patterns of emotional avoidance can help us be more aware of our patterns and make different choices that can help us be more emotionally responsive.

Working with Sticky Emotions

I wholeheartedly believe that all emotions are important. Exploring each of them and our relationship to them will be a lifelong process. For the purposes of our work, I want to spend more time with some *sticky* emotions: guilt and shame. These emotions often surface when engaging in learning and unlearning systems of oppression, which is important work in order to sustain change.

Shame and Guilt

Changing our minds or behavior can feel like a threat to what feels normal, even if our thoughts or ways of being are not helping us or others be well. This can activate a nervous system stress response. We may experience shame or guilt when we have experienced an *intention–action gap*. (more on this in Chapter 5). This may cause *cognitive dissonance*, which is the very uncomfortable experience we have when our actions are out of alignment with our beliefs and values. Recognizing the discomfort and tending to it is helpful for our growth since we are closing the gap between our intentions and our actions.

Guilt Can Support Our Growth

If we habitually avoid the discomfort of guilt, we are missing opportunities to grow and change. Our capacity to change is reliant on our ability to navigate discomfort. Change and growth are not easy. In *The Book of Forgiving: The Fourfold Path for Healing Ourselves and Our World*, Desmond Tutu (2014) wrote:

> Growth happens through obstacles and only with resistance. A tree must push up against the dirt, the solid resistance of the ground, in order to grow. Muscles grow when we apply a counterforce of resistance against them, but first they tear apart and break down, only to become even stronger in the rebuilding.
>
> *(p. 138)*

Tutu's (2014) wisdom does not promote the idea that "what doesn't kill you makes you stronger," especially when it relates to identity-based trauma and harms. His words are, however, an invitation to learn how to become less afraid of change when the change process feels uncomfortable.

Rather than run away from feeling guilty, we can choose the mindset that we have been given a gift. Accountability is a beautiful process in which we learn more about ourselves, other people, and strengthen our relationships. Guilt can increase our ability to reflect on when we have done something that negatively impacted someone else and learn from that discomfort.

Shame

bell hooks (2013) expressed that "Shaming is one of the deepest tools of imperialist, white supremacist, capitalist patriarchy because shame produces trauma and trauma often produces paralysis" (n.p.). This is also noted in Brene Brown's (2020) research in which she found that "shame has an inverse relationship with accountability" (n.p.). I don't know many people who have never experienced shaming from elders when they were young. While we may not have a clear memory of an incident, or perhaps we do, that experience and fear of social rejection lives in our bodies and likely influences how we move through the world today.

Both guilt and shame are very unpleasant experiences. Getting to know our relationship to these emotions provides insight into what is needed to move out of these emotions. Experiencing shame elicits a sense of isolation and fear (Brown, 2022; Hartling et al., 2000). Our responses to feeling shame vary based on many factors, some of which include our history of experiencing being shamed during our upbringing, our cultural upbringing, our social identities, and the power dynamics in a situation.

Brene Brown (2013) defines shame as "the intensely painful feeling or experience of believing that we are flawed and therefore unworthy of love and belonging—something we've experienced, done, or failed to do makes us unworthy of connection" (n.p.). Where shame is associated with a sense of "I am bad," guilt is the experience of "I did something bad" (Brown, 2013). This difference of labeling oneself as inherently bad versus an action/inaction or something we said/did or didn't say or do is very important.

Are You Shaming Me?

It can be difficult to distinguish between our inner experiences of shame and knowing when someone is shaming us. We may experience shame when we realize that something we have said or done has hurt or harmed someone else. Someone may share their experience of the hurt or harm we caused. They might not be shaming us, but we may perceive that they are doing so. Other times people may, in fact, be shaming us directly or indirectly, which might create a shame response within us. At times, people use shaming as a tool to control other people by threatening punishment and social rejection. Shame is used to make someone believe they are, at their core, a bad person. It is not always easy, especially in the moment, to know if we are being shamed or not. We may need to gain perspective from other people in order to make sense of a situation and be willing to be uncomfortable if their response is different from our hoped outcome.

Reflecting on Our Relationship to Shame & Guilt

Take some time to reflect on your relationship to shame and guilt. It may be helpful to use a practice from chapter one or two before starting this reflection. Take at least five minutes to reflect. You may find that you need more time than that. Use the sensations chart if it is helpful.

Shame:

- What does it feel like?
- What messages do you send to yourself?
- Where in your body do you experience it?
- What do you tell yourself when you are experiencing shame?
- Do you embrace it? Avoid it? Pretend it doesn't bother you?

Guilt:

- What does it feel like?
- Where in your body do you experience it?
- What do you tell yourself when you are experiencing guilt?
- Do you embrace it? Avoid it? Pretend it doesn't bother you?

Shame and Guilt:

- What are the similarities for you between shame and guilt?
- What are some key differences for you?
- How can you tell you are feeling shame versus guilt?

Shame and Guilt Avoidance

Linda Hartling et al. (2000) defined *strategies of disconnection/ survival*. These strategies were then adapted by Dr. Brené Brown (2018), who termed them *shame shields*, or the different ways we try to protect ourselves from experiencing shame. They are *Moving Toward*, *Moving Away*, and *Moving Against* (Brown, 2018; Hartling et al., 2000), and these responses try to prevent us from experiencing or feeling shame. The emotions and emotional responses of shame avoidance are not the only times we experience these emotions and actions; but it is helpful to understand them in the context of shame avoidant maneuvers.

We may try to push the feeling of shame away by *moving toward* the shame. We might try to engage in people-pleasing, try to be or appear perfect, and we might try to gain approval from other people around us. This is also connected to the *fawn* nervous system response. There may be other times, when we experience shame, we might *move against*. This shows up as aggression, using power-over, or attempting to counter-humiliate or shame someone (Hartling et al., 2000). It might also show up as fury, anger, or self-righteousness. It is important to differentiate between being defensive and protecting oneself from actual harm by defending oneself.

For example, if someone is being asked to address a racist or transphobic comment, and they become defensive with a blustery statement such as, "I didn't mean it like that!" or "You're being ridiculous," they are being defensive. If someone is visibly angry and saying, "I do not deserve to be talked to like that" as a result of being accosted with a slur or identity-based insult, they are defending themselves. The outward appearance may seem the same, but the origin of the anger is very different. Defensiveness isn't always obvious. Sometimes it can be a comment made with a calm demeanor like "Well, I just think we should focus on the positive and not be so negative." This deflection can appear when someone has surfaced inequities.

The other type of shame avoidance strategy is *moving away* (Brown, 2018). This is connected to the *freeze/collapse* nervous system response. In this strategy, we may withdraw, hide, be secretive, or not speak. A person in a *freeze/collapse* response may seem like they are ignoring you or "noncompliant." It may be impossible to know what is happening for someone else, but if we can approach their *freeze/collapse* response with curiosity rather than judgment, we may discover a path toward helping someone out of a freeze response. It can seem helpful to try to "shake" people out of this response; but what is needed is a calm, grounded, and gentle approach. It could sound like reminders of "I'm here when you're ready" or "I know this is hard, but we can work through this together". The tone behind those messages must match otherwise they will be meaningless.

Reflecting on Our Shame & Guilt Avoidance Strategies

Take 5–10 minutes to reflect on your shame and guilt avoidance strategies.

- Which ones do you use frequently?
- Are there different situations you use certain ones?
- Who are you more likely to use the different strategies with?
- What do each of them feel like for you?

Nervous System Responses

Emotions and sensations happen simultaneously. Depending on our levels of awareness of our body's inner sensations, or *interoception*, we may or may not have a lot of language about the sensations we experience. Just as with our ability to name our emotional experience, we can increase our ability to be aware of our inner world and make connections between our emotions and sensations. We can also layer on awareness of emotions, sensations, and our nervous system state.

The *nervous system responses & shame avoidance* chart, adapted from the work of Pat Ogden (2009), Kai Cheng Thom (2022), Dan Siegel (1999), Linda Hartling and colleagues (2000), and Brené Brown (2018), below shows the relationship between our nervous system states, sensations, thoughts, and actions and their connection to shame avoidance strategies. This is not a comprehensive list. It is a starting place to begin to reflect on your own experiences. I encourage you to make a chart or some visual of your own to begin to explore your inner world.

Nervous System Responses & Shame Avoidance

	Sensations	*Emotions*	*Thoughts*	*Actions*
Activation/ Mobilization *Moving Against Shame*	Tension Clenching Narrowed Vision Scowling Heavy Breathing Hot/Fiery	Anger Frustration Annoyance Irritation Fury Hate	I need to get out of here. How dare they?! They are (insert insults here)! This is ridiculous!	• Yelling • Banging on surfaces • Throwing • Big gestures • In other people's space • Pointing fingers
Rest and Digest	Ease Relaxation Softness Warm Spacious Zesty	Calm Happy Curious Grateful	I can handle this. I feel confident. I wonder what is happening for them. I can move through this discomfort.	• Intentional movements • Relaxed pace • Relaxed face and eyes • Steady, clear voice

	Sensations	*Emotions*	*Thoughts*	*Actions*
Fawn *Moving Toward Shame*	Small Tight Buzzy	Worried Nervous Anxious Fearful	I need to make myself small. I need to make them calm. I need to create safety. I am not safe.	• Meek voice • Slow, tentative movements • Perfectionism • People pleasing • Averting eyes • Looking down • Over-apologizing
Freeze/ Collapse *Moving Away*	Stuck Frozen Rigid Widened Eyes Rapid Breathing Cold/Icy Dense Hollow	Sad Devastated Disappointed Afraid Nervous Scared Overwhelmed Shame Hopeless	I can't move. I don't know what to do. I'm afraid.	• Head down • Immobile • Unmoving • Hiding • Jerky movements • Chest collapsed

There are times when we may be overwhelmed with our experience or a situation and try to pinpoint the source of our overwhelm. We may blame someone else for our feelings. We can learn how to become more aware of what is happening within us so we are more skillful in our emotional navigation with ourselves and in our relationships with others.

TONAL: A Practice to Navigate Emotions

In mindfulness practices, we learn how to loosen a metaphorical grip. This doesn't mean we move passively through life and accept mistreatment or ignore major issues. It means that we become aware enough of our patterns of trying to control outcomes through sheer willpower and force. Mindfulness also allows us to release emotional and mental tension, so we are clearer in our heart and mind, allowing us to see more options and make more conscious choices. Learning how to navigate emotions, particularly ones that we feel uncomfortable with, can help us move out of a stress response in which we are likely to be reactive, and toward a balanced emotional state in which we can be responsive.

TONAL can be used during a moment of heightened emotions or it can be used to reflect back on a situation and to gain more insight. We can practice TONAL in any position—sitting, standing, lying down. It may be helpful for some to move around instead of being still. Over time, it will become easier and quicker to move through this practice.

T: tune in
O: observe sensations and thoughts
N: name the emotion and experience
A: allow the emotion to move
L: loving response to self

TONAL in the Moment

First, we must acknowledge that we are having an emotional response. We need to bring our awareness by *tuning in*. This is often easier said than done, especially with high-intensity emotions like anger, shame, guilt, and overwhelm. After we tune in, *observe sensations and thoughts*.

Take note of what is happening in your body and in your mind. As you become more aware of your inner experience, start to find the emotion words that seem to be close to your experience. When you start to label your emotional experience, you can throw as many words into the mix as you like. As you start to build more *emotional granularity*, it will become easier to quickly and accurately name the most present emotion(s). Remember that it is entirely possible to feel more than one emotion at the same time. Overwhelm and frustration can coexist. Following the naming, *allow the emotion to move*.

It is important that we find a way, even if it is subtle, to move the energy of sticky emotions like frustration, anger, irritation, fear, and overwhelm. The type of movement you need will likely be different from someone else's. Generally, anger needs movement: foot tapping, rocking, deeper exhales, walking around. Fear also needs movement, but a gentler start up, such as rocking or swaying, deep pressure, like squeezing your hands, or pressing your hands on your legs, or squeezing your arm. Accessing this movement in the context of a meeting or during a class may be challenging. Find a small way to let the emotion flow so that it doesn't become trapped and stuck.

We can then offer a *loving response* to yourself. This might be "I have the right to feel this," or "My emotions are normal and I don't need to suppress them." Find words that feel authentic to you. As you build your own responses, you can think of people who have offered supportive and empathetic responses and use those phrases/words to help you find words and messages that have been helpful for you.

The Goal Is Not Perfection

Will TONAL ensure that you never snap at someone or freeze up in a tense moment? Will it be the key to always feeling happy, grateful, and relaxed? Absolutely not. That is not the goal. The goal of this practice is for us to be more aware of what is happening when it is happening and to build more opportunity for choice when it's available. There will be days and moments when you truly do not have the capacity to be fully present with your emotions. When we are sick, running on low sleep, lacking structural support in our job, or working through challenging interpersonal conflict, it is unlikely we will be able to navigate our days as skillfully as when we are well, and the days feel smooth. Be gentle with yourself.

TONAL as a Reflection Practice

There is an important distinction between dwelling in an emotion versus experiencing an emotion. That is not to say that you should never dwell in an emotion. There are many reasons why we feel stuck in an emotion. There is nothing inherently wrong with that. The same is true for the youth that we support; they may be stuck in an emotional experience. Our job with ourselves, and with those we are supporting, is not to try to pressure ourselves or someone else out of their emotional experience. Our work is how to stay present with an emotional experience so that the insight and wisdom the emotion is trying to communicate to us is revealed. Rarely does it happen as quickly as we would like.

Our memories are imperfect and that is okay. You do not need to have a photographic memory for this practice to be beneficial. One of the main differences when we use TONAL as a reflective practice is that we will be able to more fully process and express our emotions. It may even be helpful to use this with a trusted friend, partner, or loved one.

If you start to process a challenging situation and begin to re-experience the intense emotion and it feels too overwhelming, first try some of the mini-practices from Chapter 1 to return to the moment and recenter. If it continues to be too intense, it might be helpful to connect with someone who feels grounding and supportive. You use reflective TONAL as a journal practice, a silent meditative practice, or as a more embodied practice by speaking and acting out as much as is helpful.

T: Tune back in: what was the situation?
O: Observe: what sensations was I experiencing? What thoughts did I have?
N: Name: what emotions was I experiencing?
A: Allow: allow the emotion to be expressed now.
L: Loving response: what kind of loving response can I offer myself?

Begin with *tuning back in* and recall the situation and the setting, including the people. Bring as much important context as you can to mind. You can even visualize it if that is helpful. Then move to *observe* and picture yourself in that setting. Become curious about the sensations you were experiencing. Try to remember the thoughts you had. Now *name* the emotions you were experiencing. Refer to your feelings chart or feelings wheel to help name your emotional experience. Then, *allow* that emotion to be expressed now.

This part of the reflective practice can be particularly helpful if you weren't able to fully access movement during the time when your emotion was present. If you felt trapped in a meeting room, or the power dynamics in the room created a situation where you couldn't express yourself without reprimand or like you needed to keep your cool in front of youth, it is helpful to allow the movement of your emotions to flow even if they couldn't in the moment.

You can simply state your emotion out loud or you can add physical movement. These are not necessarily movements you would do in the future, but a way that you can release that held emotions energy. Anything that feels helpful (and not harmful to yourself or someone else) is wonderful. It can be curling into a ball, stomping your feet, wagging your finger, scrunching your face, making fists, shaking your whole body, standing up and walking out of a room (even if it's not the same room you couldn't leave earlier). These movements are so helpful in allowing the experience to move through our bodies, reducing our stress response, and creating a pathway for our nervous systems to return to rest and digest (Haines, 2019; Levine, 1997; Menakem, 2017). Validating our emotional experience is also supportive of releasing these pent-up emotions.

With the *loving response*, you can even say these affirmations out loud as you are allowing the movement to flow. It might sound like "I am so mad I couldn't get out of that meeting and so I am giving myself permission to stomp around right now" or "I was so frustrated during that lesson but needed to keep calm so I am giving myself the opportunity to tense my body and face now." It might feel strange, but I promise it is helpful.

We are very good at sitting with uncomfortable emotions and wanting to reflect on scenarios that went awry. That can be very helpful. However, we also need balance. You can also use this practice to reflect on a lesson or a meeting that seemed to go particularly well in which you felt joy, pride, excitement, or delight.

Emotional Navigation Affirmations:

These affirmations can support you in building a different relationship with your emotional landscape:

- My emotions are not a problem.
- I am allowed to feel all the feelings.
- My emotions have a story behind them.
- My emotions deserve space to be understood.
- I can learn new ways of being with my emotions.
- No emotions are bad even if they feel uncomfortable.

CHAPTER SUMMARY

In this chapter, we explored the origins of our relationship to our emotional landscapes: the emotions we feel comfortable expressing and the ones we do not. We also discussed the differences between shame and guilt as well as reflected on shame-avoidance strategies. We took some time to build awareness of the connection between emotional responses and our nervous system responses. The practice of *TONAL* was introduced to navigate emotions. To expand our understanding of how we relate to our own emotions, we also need to build a deeper awareness of the connection between our social identities and our socialization. Each of us was socialized to express certain emotions to suppress other emotions.

4

Exploring Social Identities

As you start this chapter, notice when you feel overwhelmed, validated, curious, frustrated, enraged, or any other emotion. Practice SOAR: *Soften, Observe, Acknowledge what is, Release judgment*, and/or TONAL: *Tune in, Observe sensations & thoughts, Name the emotion and experience, Allow the emotion to move, Loving response to self*. You can also revisit the nervous system responses & shame avoidance from the previous chapter. Before diving in, let's start with a short journal practice. Choose a medium that feels best for your processing and that is tangible so that you can revisit your reflections (handwriting, typing, voice to text, voice memo, video yourself, etc.).

Imagine you are taking a course with other educators, and you have been asked to introduce yourself to everyone. Write or video or voice record your self-introduction. You can include your current role in education and interests outside of work. Go into as much depth as you usually do in similar assignments for courses or workshops you've taken. I am intentionally leaving this quite open-ended for reasons you may already know or will know later in the chapter. Set a timer for 5 minutes, and add more time if needed. Once you have finished, set it aside but nearby, and read on.

Social Roles and Social Identities/Social Group Membership

Our identities and beliefs about our own identities and the identities of others have been shaped by many societal forces,

DOI: 10.4324/9781003540687-5

including our families, media, and the cultures we were raised in (Harro, 2018; Kirk & Okazawa-Rey, 2018; Tatum, 2018). Learning more about our own social identities and the social identities of the members of our communities is essential to understanding the dynamics within our schools and broader society. Adams and Zúñiga, (2016), describe how we learn to understand ourselves and others through *socialization*:

> Socialization refers to the lifelong process by which we inherit and replicate the dominant norms and frameworks of our society and learn to accept them as "common sense." In particular, we learn to think of social identity categories as essential and natural, and of social hierarchies as inevitable. Our socialization processes rarely point out that our norms perpetuate a world view based on the maintenance of advantage for some, relative to disadvantage for others.
>
> *(p. 44)*

People whose identities are marginalized by society are at constant risk of receiving devaluing messages about themselves. These messages are present throughout society: at home, in schools, at work, the community, the news, and other forms of media (songs, books, TV, movies, etc.). People who live with multiple identities marginalized by society are more aware of the injustices, oppressions, and inequities in our world (Lorde 2014; Hurtado 1996; Niemann 2012). The stories of people in these groups are often devalued, not believed, and/or retold and misinterpreted by people with dominant identities (e.g. White men describing what Black disabled trans women experience). These stories often overemphasis *identity* as an issue rather than focusing on the society and societal messaging that puts people in danger. One's identity is not what puts someone at risk; it is the way people are socialized to value or devalue people based on their identities.

Dominant identities are associated with more access to power and privilege. This manifests as access to a broader range of jobs, money, social value, and positive representation in the media.

Holding dominant identity/ies does not mean people have not experienced trauma(s) or received harmful messages about themselves. bell hooks (2010) wrote that "patriarchy is the single most life-threatening social disease assaulting the male body and spirit in our nation" (n.p. hooks). There is a direct link between stress, emotional and physical health, and a rigid adherence to the rules of patriarchy: being self-reliant, suppressing emotions, and exerting power over others, among other aspects, have been found to be detrimental to one's health (Scott-Samuel et al., 2015; Stanistreet et al., 2005). We are all harmed by systems of domination and that harm presents itself differently. Within each of us exists multiple social identities; some of us hold societally undervalued or marginalized identities and overvalued or dominant identities simultaneously (Adams & Zúñiga, 2016; Tatum, 2018).

Intersectionality

The term *intersectionality* was coined by Kimberlé W. Crenshaw to disrupt the oversimplification of identity and the avoidance of addressing the multiple ways in which a person could be experiencing discrimination based on their multiply societally marginalized identities (Crenshaw et al., 1995). Crenshaw, and Black feminists before her, recognized that in far too many contexts, including the legal system, you could either be Black or a woman, but not both. Those rigid boundaries could not recognize sexism and racism coexisting simultaneously. We need this level of nuance to bring more richness into understanding how our world currently operates depending on your social group memberships. For example, while White women experience sexism, they are not experiencing anti-Black racism or the racism and discrimination that Asian women, Muslim women, or trans women experience.

Intersectionality allows us to analyze the ways in which power and disempowerment, access, and denial of access to rights, privileges, and humanity, are afforded to some but not all in relation to social identity and how our socio-political world is (dis)organized. According to Patricia Hill Collins (2015), intersectionality "references the critical insight that race, class, gender, sexuality, ethnicity, nation, ability, and age operate not as unitary, mutually exclusive entities, but as reciprocally constructing phenomena that in turn shape complex social inequalities" (p. 2).

Social identities are socially constructed, meaning that "norms, ideas, and institutions that may now seem natural or inevitable grew out of specific historical or social processes" (Adams & Zúñiga, 2016). This means that categories and groups, such as race, gender, and disability, were created throughout history and served a purpose to elevate the social status and social conditions for some, while simultaneously creating barriers to access for others (Chemaly, 2018; Ho, 2015; Vaid-Menon, 2020). Our society and dominant cultural messaging inform us that some identities are more valuable and worthy, while others are deemed less valuable (Bell, 2018b; Haines, 2019; Sue, 2016).

Reflecting on Your Own Social Group Membership/Social Identities

In a conversation with James Baldwin in 1973, Nikki Giovanni offered this insight: "I found out that if you don't understand yourself, you don't understand anybody else" (p. 22). For some readers you may have grown up discussing your own social identities often at home and at school. For others, you may have little experience and/or comfort with discussing your social identities. This reflection practice will give you more insight into both your familiarity with your own social identities and why you are or are not versed in this language.

Using the chart below, take some time to reflect on your social group membership and the social identities that you do not hold. Not all identities are static or fixed; identities can be mutable and change with time (e.g., as we age, our identity and relative privilege shifts and is also connected to race and gender) and the social context we are in. Reflecting on the family structure you grew up in and how your body size has changed over the years can also help you see how not all identities are permanent while others may be more fixed.

If you are using this book in a group setting or as a group read, do not require people to share every single aspect of their identity with others. People whose identities are societally marginalized are not required to disclose identities that will increase their real and perceived risk of social harm. No one owes anyone their stories. However, for people with a dominant identity (e.g. White), it is important to move with and through the discomfort that may arise from naming that identity aloud.

Not all identities are captured in the table. If your identity is not here; add it in. For people who live within *border identities* (Adams & Zúñiga, 2016), such as mixed-race people, you will notice that you do not neatly fit into categories. There are many iterations of social identity maps and frameworks, so if this one does not work for you or your setting, don't feel pressured to use it. It is also important to note that language changes and that the words used here may not be useful and/or will be outdated at some point. Rather than adhering to rigid rules, and seeking the perfect terms, we need to be responsive to the adaptations that come from people within a particular group and community.

Take time to find your identities in the chart below. Be aware of your thoughts, emotions, and physical sensations as you move through this practice.

Social Identities

Identity type	*Identities marginalized by society*	*Dominant identities associated with power, privilege and access*
Citizenship/ documentation	People without citizenship or documentation	U.S. Citizen
Gender expression	Feminine, gender nonconforming	Masculine, Gender-conforming
Gender identity	Genderqueer, nonbinary, women, transgender	Men, Cisgender
Sexuality/sexual orientation	Asexual, Bisexual, Gay Lesbian, Pansexual, Queer	Heterosexual, allosexual, monosexual
Sex	Female, Intersex	Male
Class	Working Class, Poor	Middle & Upper Class
Religion/Spirituality	Agnosticism, Atheism, Baha'i, Buddhism, Confucianism, Hinduism, Indigenous Spiritual Traditions, Islam, Judaism, Jainism, nonreligious, Spiritism	Christianity, Catholicism

Identity type	*Identities marginalized by society*	*Dominant identities associated with power, privilege and access*
National Origin	People not from the United States	People from the United States
Disability/Ability	Disabled	Abled/non-disabled
Ethnicity	Non-Western-European American	Western-European American
Language	Languages other than English as first language, Speaking with accented English	English as first language
Age	0-34 and 56+ years old	35-55 years old
Race	People of the Global Majority, mixed race	White people
Body Size and Stature	Very tall, very short, fat	People who can: easily find clothes, can sit comfortably in chairs, cars, public transportation
Family Structure (reflect on childhood and current)	Divorced, queer, trans parents, polyamorous families, single-parents, adoptive parents, mixed racial/biological families, death of a parent, foster families, estranged from biological family	Married, monogamous, heterosexual relationship, with children or plans to have children
Level of Formal Education	Did not finish high school, earned GED, first generation college student	Educational family legacy
Carceral System	Formerly incarcerated	Not formerly incarcerated

Beverly Daniel Tatum (2018) noted that people with dominant identities (e.g., cisgender, man, White) are less likely to name those identities, whereas people whose identities have been subordinated by society will often name them (e.g. Korean, Black, gay, woman). This has been my experience in educational settings, as well. White people will often avoid saying "White" and will instead focus on their ethnic origins (e.g. Irish, French, Dutch, etc.); alternatively, they will use the term "Caucasian." The term "Caucasian" emerged from the pseudoscience of racial categorization and the belief of White racial superiority (Baum, 2006; Painter, 2010). Therefore, I do not recommend using this term because of its origins.

Adams and Zúñiga (2016) explain the differences between *social roles* and social group membership. They describe that *social roles* include "parent–child, teacher–student, doctor–patient, etc.," and they further note that "although social roles are also constructed and often are attached to power differences, they are not essentialized to the same extent as social group memberships" (p. 108). This doesn't mean that your social roles and your other identities do not hold importance; they do, and it is important to recognize that some jobs are feminized and have a workforce composed mostly of women (e.g. teachers, nurses, etc.).

These jobs are therefore frequently discounted and/or less valued by the public. We may feel pride and connection to the social roles we hold, which is beautiful, and it is still critical to name and understand our privileged/dominant identities in addition to our social roles. Return to your introduction "assignment" again. What do you notice about how you described yourself at the beginning of the chapter?

For people with dominant racial and gender identities in particular:

- Did you share any of your dominant identities?
  - If you did, *how* did you do it? Were there any hints of sarcasm or self-deprecation?
- Did you share more social roles than identities?

For people whose identities have been societally marginalized (note: these questions should **never** be used as mandatory questions people are required to answer in a group):

- Which of your identities do you feel comfortable sharing in your school/workplace?
- Which of your identities do you avoid sharing when talking about yourself to people in your school/workplace?
- How does it feel to hide parts of yourself for self-preservation and protection?

Take some time reflecting on these prompts:

- I think the most about these identities…
- I think the least about these identities…
- In our society, these identities give me the most access (privilege)…
- In our society, these identities most often deny me access (privilege)…
- I know the least about these identities of mine…
- I know the least about these identities I do not share with others…
- I was raised to believe that talking about social identities…

For readers who focused more on social roles and inadvertently avoided social identities, make a new entry. Find a way to incorporate naming your privileged racial and gender identities. Notice if sarcasm or self-deprecation emerge, since these are often indicative of discomfort. It may feel more comfortable to say something to the effect of "Well, I'm a white man, so I guess I'm just super privileged" with sarcasm rather than sitting with the realities of what that privilege means and being with that discomfort.

For people with dominant identities, these questions may be supportive in helping you build a healthy relationship with your dominant identities:

- What discomfort did/do I feel about my dominant identities?
- Are any shame avoidance strategies showing up?
- What would it be like to be curious and open to changing my views of myself and my role(s)?
- Who are some people with dominant identities that have used their social influence for justice?

If you are someone with societally marginalized identities, these questions may help you process these experiences:

- How does this knowledge help me understand what I've been through?
- What grief might I be experiencing that this is true for me and other people like me?
- What legacies are in my lineage?

A Deeper Reflection on Our Socialization and Emotional Landscape

In Chapter 3, you were invited to reflect on the emotions you were encouraged and discouraged to show outwardly. Let's take a more in-depth look at your emotional socialization. Set aside 10–15 minutes for this reflection. Use one of the foundational or mini mindfulness practices before you start. Then respond to these reflection questions.

- Were there emotions you were told were dangerous to show in front of other people?
- Were there emotions you were told were dangerous to show in front of certain people?
- Were there emotions you were taught to avoid expressing?
- Were there emotions you were taught were "healthy"?
- In your family/upbringing, were there gendered emotional expressions at home?
- In school, what emotions were acceptable?
- In school, which emotions were unacceptable?
    - What happened when someone showed "unacceptable" emotions?
- What impact has this had on you?

As you close this reflection, take some time to move around or use one of the foundational practices from Chapter 1. Going for a walk, doing a workout, taking a dance break or solo karaoke session are all wonderful options too! When you return to your reflection, take note of any themes you noticed around social identity and emotional expression.

Identity Affirmations

You can use these or any other identity-based affirmations to remind yourself that you are important and your identities matter but do not limit you.

- My identities matter.
- My identities do not limit my possibilities or potential.
- My identities influence how other people perceive me, but they do not see all of me.
- I am a unique constellation of identities.
- My identities may change over my lifetime, but I know who I am at my core.
- Shame has no place when it comes to owning my identities.

CHAPTER SUMMARY

We each have social identities. Our social identities are connected to social ideas of access to power and privilege. Although our social roles are important, social identities are different from social roles. It is beneficial to understand our social roles so we understand ourselves more and are aware of how other people may be perceiving us. Our social identities and socialization are also connected to our emotional landscape.

5

Identifying Our Values

Beliefs and Values

Our beliefs and values shape how we experience the world around us. We each hold beliefs about ourselves, other people, and our world. Beliefs are what we believe to be true about the world. We may even hold contradictory beliefs within ourselves: "people are inherently good" and "people will never change." As with emotions, our beliefs and value systems were influenced and shaped by our upbringings. If we were raised in a collectivist culture, we may believe that people need to look out for each other. Or, if we were raised in a more individualistic culture, we may believe that people need to look out for themselves and be self-sufficient. If we are mixed-culture kids, we may hold some conflicting beliefs. Our core values are the principles that guide us in life.

Our values guide us in the decisions we make unconsciously and consciously. We may feel frustrated with someone or a situation when it is out of alignment with our values. It is helpful to bring the subconscious to the level of consciousness so we are aware of why we may experience frustration, irritation, or anger with ourselves or others.

Our lived experiences with being on the receiving end of injustice or unkindness have also influenced our current value system. The values instilled in us at a young age may have been around justice and disrupting injustice. Remember that one

DOI: 10.4324/9781003540687-6

person's view of what justice is may be very different from someone else's. Other people may hold values focused on kindness, which may lead to tension when issues of accountability and addressing inequities surface. One person's expectations about kindness will not be the same for everyone. These tensions are omnipresent in our work and personal relationships. Of course, there are many other experiences that have shaped our beliefs and our values, and there are many resources out there to explore that more deeply.

Beliefs and Values Can Change

Our beliefs and values are not permanent. They can be intentionally shifted with new experiences and as we build more awareness of ourselves and the world (Russo et al., 2022). It is possible for people raised in hyper-individualistic cultures with a belief that it's every person for themselves, valuing independence to shift to a belief that we need take care of each other and a value of "interdependence" through learning, unlearning, and developing new habits.

The values we hold are also changed by the people we are around (Yudkin et al., 2021). This is particularly important because we are sometimes creatures of habit and comfort. We may seek out people who share our beliefs and values, which can reinforce our idea that our values are the epitome of morality and that they are shared by everyone. The more we expand our social circle, the more likely we are to engage in positive and prosocial change and decrease our biased perceptions (Benko, 2023).

However, these relationships must contain authentic relational depth and closeness, not surface-level friendships and/or tokenized friendships by White people with People of the Global Majority in order for these relationships to be a positive experience for both people within the relationship (Plummer et al., 2016). A couple of tokenized "friendship" phrases are "I have a (non-dominant identity) friend," and "Well, I'd like to ask my (societally marginalized identity) friend about this." These are often defensive maneuvers used when someone is asked to address racism, sexism, homophobia, transphobia, xenophobia, ableism, or any other form of othering and oppression.

Our ability to be very clear with ourselves about exactly what our beliefs and values are can help us understand ourselves and how our values may be different from someone else's. We often have clashes of beliefs and values but aren't aware of this.

Reflecting on Beliefs About Humanity

Carve out about 10–15 minutes (or more) for this reflection. This activity is best practiced as a freewriting or stream-of-consciousness exercise. This prevents us from getting stuck in our stories or trying to edit ourselves.

It may be helpful to revisit one of the mindfulness practices from chapter one or chapter two. You can also use any other form of grounding/centering practice that supports you in moving into a more relaxed and open state. Then respond to this prompt: "I believe this is generally true about people…" and write as much as you can. If you stop writing before the timer goes off, reread what you wrote, see if anything else surfaces, and write that down.

When the timer goes off, take a few minutes to move around. Don't use your phone or check your email. Take time to let the reflection settle. Move around, look outside, tidy up a space, or simply rest. Then revisit and read what you wrote. Take note of what you learned or relearned about yourself and your beliefs.

Reflecting on Core Values

A note: if you do a short internet search for "core values exercise" there will be many to explore. You are welcome to find an alternative one or list with more values if that would be helpful.

Set aside about 10–15 minutes for this reflection practice. Use one of the foundational or mini-mindfulness practices before you start. Then look at the list below. Take a few minutes to familiarize yourself with the list and look up any words that you aren't quite sure of their meaning. You can add more in the blank spaces if you would like. Then, without overthinking, circle the 15 words that you feel the strongest connection with.

Chart: List of Core Values

generosity	community	responsibility	friendship	curiosity
knowledge	compassion	security	justice	adaptability
individuality	assertiveness	learning	teamwork	leadership
authenticity	spirituality	family	toughness	moderation
status	kindness	optimism	organization	calm
improvement	dignity	discipline	self-reliance	dedication
transparency	dependability	confidence	professionalism	comfort
prosperity	health	gratitude	balance	imagination
reverence	sustainability	order	power	humility
achievement	integrity	solitude	courage	meaning
boldness	unity	contribution	skillfulness	play
freedom	structure	spontaneity	control	thoughtful
courtesy	grace	uniqueness	intelligence	logic
creativity	cleanliness	innovation	conviction	support

Write the 15 words you circled into a list. Start to group them. You might gather them into groups of three or five. Some people find three too few and others find five to be too many. Pick the number that works for you. Of your columned list of three or five, choose the one word or short phrase that best represents that group. After you have finished this, notice how you feel.

Your values influence and inform the decisions you make every single day. Becoming clear about your values and identifying when you are in or out of alignment with your values is beneficial for identifying why a situation, a conversation, or a policy within your setting creates frustration, anger, or confusion for you. This clarity can guide you toward enacting change within your sphere of influence.

We must build our capacity to grapple with the *intention–action gap* each of us has. In our hearts, we may truly care for all of our students and want them to thrive. However, there are times when our actions or inactions do not align with the intention within our hearts.

Personal Intention–Action Gaps

The distance between how we want to live and show up in our work in education and how we actually do show up is called an *intention–action gap*. Each of us may always experience moments of intention–action gaps. This is the distance between living into our core values and the actions we take daily. When I am stressed, I sometimes do not live up to my core value of compassion. I become more irritable and frustrated and often view people through a filter of impatience rather than compassion. This is part of being a complex person in a complex world.

Reflecting on Our Values & Our Intention-Action Gaps

Set aside about 10–15 minutes for this reflection practice. Prior to starting, you can revisit one of the mindfulness practices from either chapter one or chapter two or use any other form of grounding/centering practice that supports you in moving into a more relaxed and open state. Then reflect on the following prompts to build awareness of your intention–action gaps.

- How do/did my values influence my decision to work in education?
- In what ways am I living into my values each day?
- In what ways am I not living into my values each day?
- Are there values that I currently have that I would like to change or adapt?
- What is something I could do to be more aligned with my values?
- Who is someone/are some people that could be supportive of my work to be in more alignment with my values?
- Who is someone/are some people that could be supportive of my work as I change/adapt my values?

After finishing your reflection, take some time to move around or rest. Stretch, walk, dance, gaze out the window, lay down on the couch. Then return and read your response. Notice how your body feels and the emotions that are surfacing.

Values Affirmations

- My values can guide me.
- My values can change.
- My beliefs about people can change.
- I do not need to have the same values as other people.
- I do not need to convince other people that they should have my values.
- I can understand myself and others better when I know my own values and theirs.

CHAPTER SUMMARY

In this chapter, we explored some of our personal beliefs and core values. Holding an awareness of our personal values can help us notice where there are intention–action gaps. Beliefs and values can change and are influenced by the people who make up our community. Taking note of who is influencing you and your value system can be a way to close your intention-action gap and expand your worldview.

6

Are We Well?

Contextualizing the Chaos

I have no doubt that you chose to work in education because of your values and your passion to make a difference in this world; nearly every educator I have encountered has said some version of this. There are many educators who talk about how much they are energized by working with youth and the joy it brings them. At the same time, they express immense frustration with the system as a whole and the pressures they feel to do more with less. Holding the complexity that two things that are seemingly oppositional can be true at the same time is essential to more fully understanding ourselves and our world. We will continue to dwell in the paradoxes and multiple truths of working in education in other parts of this book.

We can believe in education and be disillusioned by the state of education. We can love our work with youth and feel exhausted by the work. We can hope that education can be a place for belonging and growth, and we can believe that our educational spaces are negatively impacting people. We need to hold these contradictions to gain an honest perspective of our world.

The pace of a school day and the entire school year is fast. Urgency is omnipresent. As you read the next statements notice how your body feels, the emotions and thoughts that surface. It may be helpful to use a feelings chart/wheel and/or sensations chart.

DOI: 10.4324/9781003540687-7

- *We have to get through this lesson plan to make sure we can get to the next one on time.*
- *We need to move through this unit before school break.*
- *All of my students should be meeting grade level by the end of this year.*
- *We need our preschools to be ready for kindergarten.*
- *We need our kindergarteners ready for first grade.*
- *We need to get our high school students ready for the "real world".*
- *We need to get through this meeting.*

And on and on it goes. No wonder it is hard to feel a sense of groundedness. How does your body feel in this moment?

During times of intense overwhelm, we may find ourselves swept into a vortex of chaos. This vortex pulls us in, and we lose our sense of self. It is impossible to tell how distressed we are until we can take a moment to pause and notice what is happening internally. The inside of the vortex all feels the same, so we may not even notice when we have reached the top and are far removed from our sense of ground.

The vortex feeds on and fuels chaos, intensity, urgency, sharpness, knee-jerk reactions, competition, scarcity, rigidity, frustration, impatience, and over-simplicity. When most of our society is organized around urgency and intensity, it can be challenging to recognize the state we are actually in. Our habits feel familiar, and even when habits are unhelpful, we crave familiarity, especially when we have external overwhelm (like working in a school). Everyone around us is also swept up into this chaos, and they seem fine. So everything must be fine, right? Or is it?

This isn't to say that we don't need urgency and to act urgently at times. The issue is when urgency becomes our overriding way of moving through the world, and we react urgently to everything. When our nervous system stays in a state of high intensity, and it becomes nearly impossible to discern between urgent and non-urgent.

The perpetual swirling motion of a vortex doesn't create room for compassion, curiosity, patience, ease, slowness, gentleness, curiosity, hope, creativity, joy. We can begin to find our connection back to groundedness once we recognize we are, indeed, in a vortex. We will need other people, too. They can help us, and we can help them get out of the swirling mess. We need each other and we need to make sense of the vortex we have been pulled into.

Our Nervous Systems

Our nervous systems are incredibly complex and fascinating. Dan Siegel (1999) coined the phrase *window of tolerance* to describe how our nervous systems respond to different environmental factors. Pat Ogden et al. (2006) and Pat Ogden (2009) used this framework in conjunction with mindfulness to support people healing from traumatic events. Kai Cheng Thom (2022) adapted this further to reflect how these nervous system states are present in conflict, particularly conflict at the intersection of social justice and trauma-healing work. We explored this concept earlier in Chapter 3 as it relates to shame avoidance.

We need our nervous systems to be responsive to our environment and even reactive when the situation needs that level of response. When people are under constant stress, the nervous system adapts to this stress level and our internal perception of our baseline becomes distorted. What feels "normal" does not necessarily mean this "normal" is supporting our health and well-being.

We have all said something regrettable to a student, a colleague, or toward ourselves. Increasing our self-awareness through mindfulness practices and reflection has the potential to build our capacity to be more responsive rather than reactive. The chart below shows our nervous system states and sensations we may experience in those states. Take a moment to read and feel into your own nervous system. These responses are normal and we should not strive to eradicate them in ourselves or anyone else.

Nervous System State	*Sensations*
Mobilization *fight/flight*	Agitated, impatient, frustrated, furious, angry, outraged
Window of Capacity *rest/digest*	Flexible, curious, compassionate, connected to self and others, relaxed, safe
Appease *fawn*	Afraid, nervous, worried, fear of rejection
Immobilization *freeze/collapse*	Stuck, frozen, trapped

We are constantly incorporating information from our sensory world and responding to it without being consciously aware of this information-filtering. We would be cognitively exhausted if we were processing all this information consciously. Our nervous systems take in information about the environment and determine if we are safe or in danger. For some of us, our nervous systems are in hyperdrive, over-identifying stress and danger where there is not. This state is referred to as *hyperarousal*. Other nervous systems are in what is called a *hyporesponsive* state, where we underestimate situations that could be dangerous or stressful.

When we perceive a threat to our safety, our nervous systems may react by flooding our body with adrenaline and cortisol. We are taking in information regarding a variety of types of safety, including psychological safety, emotional safety, and physical safety.

Remember that each person will be responding to environmental cues differently based on their own histories and interpretations of what feels safe to them. These differences become very complicated when engaging in conversations around oppression and privilege. There will be more on this in Chapters 7, 8, and 9. For now, let's continue to explore our nervous system responses.

Our sympathetic nervous system activates when we perceive a threat to safety. We may go into an *activation/mobilization* response, also known as *fight or flight*. In this state, we may experience an increased heart rate, breathe heavier, clench our jaws, make fists, furrow our brow, and our eyes may narrow. We may experience rage, anger, frustration, indignation. This is when we might storm out of a meeting, yell at a student to get out of our classroom, or, through clenched teeth, say, "You need to go to the peace place" to a student with whom we feel frustrated. In this state we may even feel this sense of "I need to put this person in their place."

When we are in a state of *rest and digest*, we are able to take in information, to learn, to grow, to be challenged, and to greet those challenges with curiosity and courage. We are aware of ourselves and connected to the other people around us. In this state we embody humility and can receive feedback without collapsing into a shame spiral.

On the other end of the sympathetic nervous system response, we may go into *immobilizatio*n or a *freeze/collapse* response. In a freeze/collapse response our shoulders may sag, we may avert our eyes, and our body may feel sluggish and like we're wearing a weighted vest or blanket. The breath may become very shallow. We may feel trapped and experience a sense of panic or even have a panic attack. To an outside observer we may appear nonresponsive and "noncompliant." There is another nervous system response called *appeasement* or *fawn*.

The *appeasement/fawn* nervous system response is when we try to create safety by appeasing another person or other people. This may sound like a high-pitched "sure" when our supervisor asks us to add another responsibility to our plate. It might be used when a brash colleague is raising their voice and we get quiet or try to ease the tension by making a joke. This response often shows up as people pleasing and attempting to achieve perfectionism.

Recognizing our nervous system responses is beneficial in being aware of how and *why* we are responding to situations. With high levels of ongoing exposure to stress, our nervous systems may become overloaded. This cumulative stress can wreak havoc on our emotional, physical, and mental health. We may be short-tempered, feel numb, act impulsively, feel disconnected from other people, have digestion issues, experience chronic pain or headaches, among other presentations of cumulative stress.

Trauma Exposure Response

Schools and school systems are rife with experiences that can lead to a *trauma exposure response*. In her 2009 book *Trauma Stewardship: Trauma Stewardship: An Everyday Guide to Caring for Self While Caring for Others*, van Dernoot Lipsky wrote that:

> A trauma exposure response may be defined as the transformation that takes place within us as a result of exposure to the suffering of other living beings or the planet. This transformation can result from deliberate or inadvertent exposure, formal or informal contact, paid or volunteer work.
>
> *(p. 41)*

A *trauma exposure response* is connected to three different origins: personal, organizational, and societal (van Dernoot Lipsky & Burke, 2009).

The personal is reflected in our "own histories and personal connections" with and in relation to trauma. If a student of ours is having ongoing medical care, our personal experiences with medical trauma, for example, may elicit strong responses within us. Our personal experiences with racial or other identity-based trauma may heighten our nervous system responses when we witness or hear about a student's experience. These personal connections are not problematic; they are just something to be aware of. If we begin to feel swept into a high state of overwhelm when trying to support someone else whose experience matches our own, we may need to seek outside resources or invite other colleagues to support the process. We don't need to try to go it alone.

The second origin of a *trauma exposure response* is organizational. Van Dernoot Lipsky and Burke (2009) identified a high demand in combination with insufficient or inadequate resources as one element of organizations contributing to a *trauma exposure response*. The other components are "lack of accountability and unethical behavior" (p. 25). The denial or rationalization of unethical behavior within an organization also contributes to, or exacerbates, a *trauma exposure response.*

The third origin of a *trauma exposure response* is societal. Living in a world that is organized by oppression in which some people have more access to their essential needs and humanity being honored than others contributes to a *trauma exposure response.* All of these co-occur and we are experiencing all origins of a *trauma exposure response* each day. When we experience and witness the impact of schools being under-funded, under-resourced, racially segregated, and subjected to ongoing public scrutiny, we are inevitably going to experience a *trauma exposure response.* There is also a demand placed on educators to perform unrealistic feats and to push youth in their care through these unhealthy and dysfunctional systems. It is no wonder our nervous systems are overloaded.

Nervous System Overload

In 2020, shortly after the emergence of COVID-19 and the subsequent global lockdown, van Dernoot Lipsky released an updated visual depicting the presentations of a trauma exposure response. This updated version combined a *trauma exposure response* and *overwhelm* from her book *Trauma Stewardship: An Everyday Guide to Caring for Self While Caring for Others* into one graphic and is titled "When Experiencing Trauma and Overwhelm." The original graphic can be found at https://traumastewardship.com/. The update highlights the ways that chronic stress, overwhelm, and *trauma exposure response* are not discrete experiences from each other; they overlap and intersect. All of these are normal responses to experiencing trauma, overwhelm, and/or a trauma exposure response. Remembering that these experiences are normal responses can create an easier pathway for compassion toward ourselves and others, rather than fear or judgment.

Take some time and look at the list of responses that may surface when experiencing trauma, overwhelm, or a trauma exposure response. As you read each one, notice how your body and heart respond. Take note of your thoughts.

When Experiencing Overwhelm and Trauma

Loneliness/isolation/ strained relationships	Feeling helpless, hopeless and that one can never do enough	Anger & cynicism (can also show up as dry sarcasm)
Addictions	Hypervigilance (always on alert) and always serious	Guilt/fear/complicated grieving
Lack of awe (nothing, even beautiful events in nature seems to evoke awe)	Sense of persecution (everyone is out to get me)	Fight/flight/immobility response
Dissociate moments (feeling out of one's body)	Inability to see options and diminished creativity	Physical ailments, depression, anxiety and other mental health experiences
Chronic exhaustion and saturated nervous system	Pulled toward confirmation bias and away from critical thinking	Lack of presence/ deliberate avoidance/ cognitive overload
Intense/rigid/ controlling/ unable to embrace complexity	Disheartened and dispirited	Grandiosity (I am better than/superior to everyone else)
Negativity bias and not assuming well	Difficulty empathizing. Minimizing/ numbing emotions	Sub-impeccable/toxic and compromised impulse control (struggle to be responsive to our stress and may instead do impulsive things like online shop or display road rage, engage in other risky social behavior, etc.)

Adapted from © The Trauma Stewardship Institute. All Rights Reserved. Used with Permission.

It is so important to not pathologize oneself or someone else for experiencing these responses. It is also not helpful to compare our experiences to someone else's, to legitimize or delegitimize our own or someone else's reality. As Resmaa Menakem (2017) reminds us:

> Trauma is not a flaw or a weakness. It is a highly effective tool of safety and survival. Trauma is also not an event. Trauma is the body's protective response to an event—or

> a series of events—that it perceives as potentially dangerous. This perception may be accurate, inaccurate, or entirely imaginary.
>
> *(p. 7)*

Our responses will differ depending on our histories, our lived experiences, and our social identities (van Dernoot Lipsky & Burke, 2009; Menakem, 2017). People also respond to the same potentially trauma-inducing or overwhelming situation or series of events differently (Haines 2019; Levine 1997; Menakem 2017). Leaving room for difference is always beneficial. There is no universal truth as to how people respond to overwhelm and/or trauma.

Reflecting on Overwhelm in My World

Use any mindfulness/grounding/centering practice that supports you in moving into a more relaxed and open state. Be aware of your thoughts, emotions, and physical sensations as you move through. Use a feelings wheel/chart and/or sensations list to help you process as needed. Then reflect on the following prompts:

- Do I see myself reflected in the chart?
- How does it feel to put a label to my experiences?
- Do I see people I work with reflected in the chart?
- Do I see students/youth reflected in the chart?
- How can this help me understand myself and other people with more curiosity and compassion?

"I love my job; I can't be burnt out..."

There have been many times throughout my career in education where I was experiencing some combination of a *secondary trauma response/trauma exposure response*, moral injury, and/or burnout. It wasn't just me; it was most of my colleagues. We attended many workshops and in-house professional development sessions about how to deal with burnout and "compassion fatigue." While researching resources for this book, I came across a folder from a 2011 "teacher wellness" training. The folder had an entire list of strategies to relax, and not one of those strategies addressed the system that is creating burnout.

Educators are often overworked and underpaid, two of the top contributors to burnout (Jotkoff, 2022; Kariou et al., 2021). This phenomenon is viewed as normal for feminized work, work that is viewed as care and work and predominantly occupied by women (Hackman, 2023). It can seem daunting or impossible to address burnout in a system that is so multilayered in complexity. Educators are overworked in a stress-inducing system.

There seems to be no limit to the external stressors placed upon the education system and everyone impacted by the system, including certified educators, non-certified educators, administrators, students, families, the broader community. Funding for education faces ongoing scrutiny, and funding is systematically moved away from high-poverty areas and predominantly Black and migrant communities. School buildings are in a constant state of disrepair, and while there seems to always be money to be found for some schools for maintenance and improvement, while money seems to disappear for other schools. These realities, in addition to the many demands of working in education, contribute to burnout.

Burnout

Maslach and Leiter (2016) summarized the six origins of workplace burnout: a) work overload, b) a lack of control to "influence decisions that affect their work, to exercise professional autonomy, and to gain access to the resources necessary to do the job," c) "insufficient recognition and reward (whether financial, institutional, or social)," d) dysfunctional community including: lack of support and trust and unresolved conflict, e) the absence of equity and social justice and fairness, and f) "a gap between individual and organizational values" (p. 105). Pause for a moment to think about your workplace. Are these origins of workplace burnout present in your school/school system? What does that mean for you and for the system as a whole?

Many educators, especially educators engaged in social justice work, often feel an overwhelming sense of urgency and are daunted by the amount of change that needs to be made in order for justice to be present (Gorski & Chen, 2015; Kotowski et al., 2022). *Burnout* is a systemic issue, not a personal failure (Maslach & Leiter, 2016). Maslach and Leiter (2016), who researched burnout in the 1970s, describes burnout as "a psychological syndrome emerging as a prolonged response to chronic interpersonal stressors on the job" (p. 103). The components of burnout are: "overwhelming exhaustion, feelings of cynicism and detachment from the job, and a sense of ineffectiveness and a lack of accomplishment" (p. 103). Pause. Take a moment. Does this feel familiar to you? If not, do you see people you work with experiencing these burnout responses?

Moral Injury

While the term *moral injury* is relatively new (Shay, 1991), the phenomenon has been discussed across various cultures throughout human history (Brock & Lettini, 2012). In the modern era this phenomenon was studied when psychologists were working with post-combat veterans, and realized that some of the distress veterans were experiencing could not be explained only by post-traumatic stress responses. In more recent years, researchers began to identify moral injury happening across professions in the healthcare industry and in education.

Dean et al. (2019) define moral injury as happening "when we perpetrate, bear witness to, or fail to prevent an act that transgresses our deeply held moral beliefs" (p. 400). We are likely to experience moral injury when we experience a sense of betrayal of what we consider to be "right" from someone in a position of authority or ourselves (Litz et al., 2009; Shay, 1991).

When people are in stressful situations and are mandated by authority figures to act in ways they wouldn't otherwise, or when they are bearing witness to harm occurring and are prevented from taking action, this can create moral injury. People experiencing moral injury may feel guilt, depression, a sense of worthlessness, remorse, despair, hopelessness, helplessness, and emotionally isolated (Brock & Lettini, 2012; Volunteers of

America, 2020). Moral injury is an incredibly common experience and something that is underdiscussed in the world of education.

In education, because of the hierarchies in place, educators and administrators are at a high risk of experiencing moral injury. Levinson (2015) highlighted different kinds of injustices that increase the risk of educators experiencing moral injury:

> *contextual injustices*: historical and/or present-day injustices beyond the school, such as poverty, trauma, lack of health care, and racial and economic segregation. Just action is further inhibited by *school-based injustices*, including discriminatory school policies and insufficient resources, training, and professional supports for educators.
>
> *(p. 211)*

As described earlier, moral injury originates from enacting something, or being unable to prevent something, that was outside of our core values/moral code. Below are some scenarios that could lead to someone experiencing moral injury. Before you read the following scenarios, I encourage you to take some time to settle your nervous system. Return to some of the foundational practices in Chapter 1, or use any other practice that is helpful for you. As you read them, notice your psychological and emotional responses. Take breaks if you need them.

Scenarios

1. *A teacher is directed to move through a rigorous math program, although most of the students in their classroom are not ready to "move on." The teacher has expressed to their curriculum director, their principal, and even the superintendent that they have never seen this group of students seem so distressed. The teacher is told to "be a team player" and that "your colleagues seem to be doing just fine with it. Why don't you ask them why you're having such a hard time following this program?" After three months of no changes, they decide to deviate from the program. Students are no longer showing any distress and are making amazing progress. The teacher is visited by the principal and reprimanded for being "behind schedule."*

2. *A para educator is told they need to learn how to physically restrain a student who throws crayons when they are upset. This para educator has strong beliefs that physical restraint is traumatizing and that there are more effective ways to support this student. They have been successful 80% of the time when they have talked soothingly and empathetically to the student, who will often then break down in tears after their burst of frustration. On multiple occasions, they have had to watch their colleagues physically restraint this student. In the middle of the school year, the para educator is told by their supervisor, who is a special educator, and their principal, that they will no longer be able to work with this student if they do not get trained in restraint.*
3. *A crisis prevention team meets weekly to discuss student behavior data and actions based on data. A member of the team, Nora, begins to notice that "disruption and defiance" is the most common referral justification, and that the students referred by educators are usually Black, receiving special education, and/or are experiencing poverty.*
4. *At the grade-level team meeting, an art teacher says she is going to call Child Protective Services because a student has been frequently absent. The classroom teacher, one of the only educators of the Global Majority in the school, knows this family and the student well. They remind the whole team that this student has chronic gastrointestinal discomfort and was recently hospitalized. The classroom teacher shares that both parents have been in regular contact with them and has been getting homework and updates sent home. The art teacher says it doesn't matter, and that it's the "responsibility as a mandated reporter to report things that are unsafe." The classroom teacher points out that there are two other students, whose parent are White and upper-middle class, have also missed a lot of school because of "educational vacations" they go on with their family. Most of the team members present say the circumstances are different. The classroom teacher points out that the family they want to report is Black, and the other families are White. Multiple team members, all of whom are White, say "this isn't about race." The decision made at the end of the meeting is that the art teacher, with the support of the guidance counselor and principal, will call CPS.*

Pause and Reflect

Use any mindfulness/grounding/centering practice that supports you in moving into a more relaxed and open state. Be aware of your thoughts, emotions, and physical sensations as you move through. Use a feelings wheel/chart and/or sensations list to help you process as needed. Then reflect on the following prompts:

1. What did I think and feel as I read these?
2. What are some situations that lead me to experience moral injury?
3. How does understanding moral injury help me in thinking about how I am feeling about my work?

Evading Change: Individualizing and Minimizing Burnout, Moral Injury and Overwhelm

When awareness of the Adverse Childhood Experiences (ACEs) study began to increase in education, unhelpful uses of ACEs began to emerge. Staff were asked to complete an ACEs screening tool and to even share their results with each other. In addition to being a huge breach of confidentiality and encouraging oversharing of incredibly personal information, the ACEs study was never designed to be used in this way. The original ACEs study also did not include experiences such as historical oppression, racism and other forms of discrimination in the present day; both important aspects of understanding and contextualizing trauma and trauma responses (Dhaliwal, 2016; Goldstein et al., 2021). Similarly, assessment tools used to measure burnout can also be misused.

In 1981, the Maslach Burnout Inventory (MBI) was developed by Dr. Christina Maslach and Dr. Susan E. Jackson. Since 1981, many variations and adaptations of the MBI have surfaced. At times, the use of the MBI or similar assessment tools have been used in ways that support a hyper-focus on individuals rather than the system. Maslach and Leiter (2021) asserts that "the MBI was designed for discovery—both of new information that extends our knowledge about burnout and of possible strategies for change" (n.p.). If you are in a leadership position, formal or informal, this intention is particularly important to remember.

Since burnout and moral injury are systemic problems, they need systemic solutions. Maslach and Leiter (2016) stated that:

> the biggest challenge I find right now is that people keep thinking of burnout as a personal problem, and how do we get people to fix themselves? What that means is, we're not paying attention to all of the causes of the problem.
>
> *(n.p.)*

Similarly, Dean et al. (2019) emphasized that "Moral injury locates the source of distress in a broken system, not a broken individual, and allows us to direct solutions at the causes of distress" (p. 401).

Take a moment to reflect on burnout in your school/school system. How has burnout been discussed, if at all? What about moral injury? Even if you have not had direct conversations or professional training on burnout or moral injury, have you heard, overheard, or received any of these kinds of messages?

- *Well, working in schools is just demanding.*
- *Maybe they just aren't cut out to work in education.*
- *Well, they really ought to just focus more on what is working instead of always complaining.*
- *Well, I'm not burned out, so I don't really think we have a problem here.*
- *This is just how we do things in education.*
- *Clearly, they just don't care about consequences for students.*
- *Educators who love what they do are just willing to go the extra mile.*

After reading those statements, take a moment to reflect on what those messages communicate and the impact they have on a school culture.

Burnout is indicative of an unsustainable pace and unhealthy work environment. Moral injury is an inevitable experience because we are complex people living in a world that doesn't always align with our inner compass. In addition to these realities, schools and school systems are often organized around "grind culture" (Hersey, 2022). The combination of this cultural pressure to do more in a profession that has high levels of secondary trauma response wreaks havoc on our nervous systems.

Mandated Wellness Is Not the Answer

A few years ago, during the early years of COVID-19, I offered an online workshop series about trauma-informed and anti-oppressive work to a school district. During a planning meeting with members of leadership, I talked about the content of my next presentation: self-care. There was a long silence. I asked the group what the silence meant. Some of the leadership team then shared that there was a high level of frustration among many staff because of the ways self-care had been approached.

They shared with me that some of the other leaders, who were not present at this meeting, were mandating "wellness" time. They required that staff go for a walk during their planning time or to engage in some other group activity that was pitched as "promoting wellness." With this background information, I changed the direction of my presentation.

We explored the tenets of trauma-informed care which included discussing the differences between "collaboration and mutuality;" "empowerment, voice, and choice" (SAMHSA, 2014); and coercion and forced group activities. One person courageously named the thing that needed to be named and said to the entire zoom room that the "mandated wellness" was actually making them unwell and stressing them out. Rather than offering a sense of wellness, it created resentment and frustration. This person shared that people needed that time to plan, prepare, and decompress. People wanted the choice about what they did with that time, not be required to engage in an activity they did not choose and did not find to be relaxing. They also shared that there was perpetual toxic positivity and avoidance of engaging in conversations about employee stress. In the closing prompt for our session, I invited participants to share what stuck with them from the presentation. The zoom chat was filled with gratitude and relief of being seen, feeling heard, and being validated.

After this session, I received a terse email from a member of leadership—one of the ones who had required these wellness activities—saying they wanted to schedule a meeting with me. I asked for more information as to the purpose of the meeting. They responded that they wanted to talk about the "very negative turn the presentation took." I responded and asked for specific examples and informed them that I would need to bill for any hours beyond the contract. I received no response. That leader's belief that the meeting was "negative" and not "productive" highlighted the mentality they had regarding sharing power.

This example is one of many instances where likely well-intentioned leaders make decisions on behalf of people without collaboration. This is a form of power-over that people in power struggle to recognize. They may believe that "it's in people's best interest, so it's okay." Regardless of the intention, this is a form of enacting power over others that is consistent with a leadership style that is unhealthy for schools and school systems. We will explore this further in the next chapter.

While mandated wellness initiatives may seem like a good idea, they are not addressing the sources of burnout or moral injury. We need shifts at all levels. We must first be aware and honest with ourselves about the impact our work and workplace has on us and the people around us. Without honesty, and without addressing the origins of burnout and moral injury, attempts to alleviate them will not work. If we have a wilting potted plant and assume it needs water, but the roots are waterlogged, we are making the problem worse.

If a wellness initiative is more focused on the optics rather than the issue, this will only increase the frustration people are feeling. Posters and "cutesy wellness" (Venet, 2021) take energy that could be better spent toward meaningful change.

Reflecting on Our Workplace Culture

The cultural context of your school or workplace impacts your well-being, or the lack of it. These reflection prompts below may be easy to respond to now. They might not. You might find it helpful to think about these over the course of a few weeks.

As you ponder these questions, notice emotional responses that surface. Take a moment to reflect on these questions to get a fuller sense of how your work place demonstrates care or is contributing to burnout and overwhelm:

- When you take a wellness or mental health day, do you feel guilty?
- When you are sick, do you come to work anyway?
- If you need to take time away from work, do you feel supported?
- If someone takes multiple sick days, how are they talked about by colleagues or administration?
- If someone takes multiple sick days, is there a system of support to ensure they are getting what they need?
- Who are the educators who receive the most praise and recognition? Do they work long, after-contracted work hours?
- How are educators who do not respond to email after contracted work hours talked about by colleagues?
- Is there equitable treatment of staff when people need time away? Do some people get preferential treatment?
- What are the unwritten or written expectations about taking work home, including responding to emails?

Take some time to notice how you feel after reflecting on these questions. This is a small list of suggestions on ways that burnout and moral injury can be directly addressed.

- Discourage people from working through lunch breaks and responding to emails after school hours
- Ensure people have adequate planning time and access to bathroom breaks
- Advocate for livable wages for everyone working within the system
- Develop collaborative solutions to the staffing shortages and substitute position shortages with staff and the community

What else would you add to this list? What would support your workplace in feeling more caring and supportive in mitigating burnout and moral injury? In the next chapter, we will identify and analyze the ways power operates with your school/school system and how *power over* contributes to burnout and moral injury. This kind of power also prevents necessary growth and change.

Affirmations to Navigate Overwhelm, Burnout, and Moral Injury

- My overwhelm/burnout does not mean I am weak; it means I am human.
- I am allowed to pause.
- Burnout is not a *me* problem; it is much bigger than me.
- I can work on identifying root causes of my burnout.
- I might not be able to change the whole system causing burnout, but I can influence change.
- I have the right to say no to practices that are hurting or harming other people.

CHAPTER SUMMARY

We live in a very overstimulating world that pressures us toward urgency and doing more with less. Schools and school systems are sites of burnout, moral injury, and *trauma exposure responses/secondary trauma responses*. Learning to understand our responses to working in a system that is overwhelming, and, at times, incongruent with our morals and values, can help us move out of self-blame and contextualize our suffering.

7

Reflecting on Power in the System

Reflecting on Power in the System

Each of us inherently has power. Just like emotions, power itself is not a problem; the way power is wielded can become a problem. We live within societal systems that promote and normalize power being used to control others. This normalization seeps into our schools. Taking time to analyze the way power is used within a school and/or workplace is essential in becoming aware of how power is used to either interrupt inequities or to sustain them. In this chapter, we will contextualize power within your school or school system. As you move through this chapter, I encourage you to notice your emotional responses and to pause and reflect throughout.

Power Balances Are Omnipresent

Many schools and educational organizations are hierarchical. People at the top make decisions for those lower down in the hierarchy. The higher you are in the hierarchy, the more influence you have over other people.

The people who most frequently make policy changes and make demands of educators and the educational system are often the least impacted by those policies. Take, for example, a group of researchers in the academy, who have only worked in partnership with educators but not as educators in a preK-12 setting,

DOI: 10.4324/9781003540687-8

developing curricula and "best practices" without meaningful relationships with educators, students, and families. This group of experts then make recommendations to federal and state government policymakers, and these suggestions do not adequately reflect the realities of working in a school or the needs of students and families. Educators are then expected to comply with these rigid policies that do not meet the needs of anyone in the system.

The people at the top, or close to the top, of the hierarchy, require those at the lower rungs to comply with and implement policies, procedures, and practices that may be contributing to moral injury, burnout, and harm more broadly. The dysfunction can become so commonplace that it becomes harder to recognize as time goes on. The people who recognize the issues often become burnt out (Gorski & Chen, 2015) and stay in jobs that wreak havoc on their well-being (Lipsky & Burke, n.d.; Nagoski & Nagoski, 2020; Robinson et al., 2019). The people who are attempting to change the system from within may become so disillusioned and dispirited by the lack of systemic change that they leave (Association & Others, 2022; Kotowski et al., 2022). This then results in the people, whose perspectives are most needed in order to create change, being pushed out (Chambers, 2025; Jotkoff, 2022).

Sandra Bloom (2013) noted that "there is always a tendency in institutions, and in the larger containing society, to regress to simple, hierarchical models of authority as a way of preserving a sense of security and stability" and that "authoritarian leadership is likely to encourage the same leadership style throughout the organization" (pp. 145–146). In schools, this pattern can be seen as building administrators mandating that educators adhere to policies such as dress codes and/or behavior interventions that are rooted in racism, classism, cisheterosexism, and ableism. In turn, educators enact authoritarian models in their work with students.

In his book, *Controlling Our Children: Hegemony and Deconstructing the Positive Behavioral Intervention Support Model*, Thomas Knestrict (2018) wrote:

> The political pressure to produce obedient, heteronomous workers is still strong and is the reason we have a paced, standardized curriculum and made the school

> culture test heavy. Data and test scores provide empirical but biased proof that students are learning and our tax dollars are being wisely spent.
>
> *(p. 83)*

This pressure is felt in schools when states monitor a narrow view of "progress" via scores on standardized assessments and pressure districts/supervisory unions to increase their performance. From this pressure, the administrators make decisions on behalf of a staff without meaningful input from the staff. Feeling this pressure, educators then make decisions on behalf of students without meaningful input from students or families. Curriculum changes, behavior policies, even unofficial changes to how individualized education programs (IEPs) are implemented, are often made without involvement from the people most impacted.

Identifying and Disrupting Power Over in the Broader System

In "A New Weave of Power, People and Politics: The Action Guide for Advocacy and Citizen Participation," Lisa VeneKlasen and Valerie Miller (2007) describe *power over* as the exertion of control and/or force on another/others. The underlying belief is that a person in a position of power is more knowing/knowledgeable and has the right to tell other people how to be in the world. This type of power promotes and encourages conformity and upholds unjust status quo.

To feel a sense of belonging within a system of *power over*, one must think, act, and perform according to the standards of the person or people in power. *Power over* relies on a rigid view of what is right and wrong and denies opportunities for dissenting perspectives. Students who do not conform are sent to the principal's office. Educators who do not conform are written up for "not being a team player." The people most likely to be targeted for noncompliance in a *power over* system are people whose identities are societally marginalized and/or people who disrupt and challenge power over leading and teaching. The educational pedagogy most utilized in a power over system is the "banking model of education" (Freire, 1978/2018).

The "banking model of education" is a model of education in which, teachers are viewed as all-knowing beings and students are empty vessels who need teachers to fill their empty minds. Students are treated as unknowing and in need of firmness. There are some educators who believe this model is necessary and beneficial and are actively employing it. However, there are other educators who may unknowingly be acting out this type of model without being aware of what they are doing. In her book *Teaching Community: A Pedagogy of Hope*, bell hooks (2004) offered this powerful reminder: "to build community requires vigilant awareness of the work we must continually do to undermine all the socialization that leads us to behave in ways that perpetuate domination" (p. 36).

Three Forms of Power Over

Lisa VeneKlasen and Valerie Miller (2007) describe three different levels of power over: *visible power, hidden power*, and *invisible power*. The first is *visible power*, in which decision-making is observed through "the formal rules, structures, authorities, institutions, and procedures of decision making…elections, political parties, laws, legislatures, corporate policy, by-laws, etc." (p. 47). In educational organizations, these are the policies adopted by school boards, the school "handbooks," and state and federal level laws and policies.

Hidden power operates when "certain powerful people and institutions maintain their influence by controlling who gets to the decision-making table and what gets on the agenda" (VeneKlasen & Miller, 2007, p. 47). This hidden power "works to hide problems and influence the agenda by controlling access to information. If people are unaware of a problem, they are unable to make informed choices or participate in public decisions that can lead to its solution" (p. 47). The authors assert that "for marginalized communities, being denied information can reinforce feelings of powerlessness, ignorance, and self-blame, but it also can spur people to action" (p. 48). Hidden power is present in schools when a student union group, only made up of students from middle- and upper-middle class backgrounds, meet and make recommendations for change without involving other students. It shows up when there has been persistent disproportionality in the suspension rates for Black, disabled and/or poor students, but these data are not shared with students or families.

The third type of power over is *invisible power*, which is insidious and omnipresent in our society. This type of power over means that "significant problems and issues are not only kept from the decision-making table, but also from the minds and consciousness of the different players involved, even those directly affected by the problem" (VeneKlasen & Miller, 2007, p. 47). The authors further note that "processes of socialization, culture, and ideology perpetuate exclusion and inequality by defining what is normal, acceptable, and safe" (p. 49). This type of power prevents issues such a racism, sexism, homophobia, transphobia, ableism, and all other forms of oppression, from being part of our collective consciousness.

As we explored in the social group membership chapter, we have all been influenced by cultural messages that shape our ideas about "normalcy." These messages attempt to prevent people, whose identities have been and are marginalized by society, to even know that they have been actively marginalized. This also supports the denial of the realities of oppression by people with positional and identity-based power. One example of *invisible power* is present in textbooks that portray the Civil Rights Movement as the "end" of racism. All of these forms of power over can and must be addressed and they impact the climate and culture of a school.

Reflecting on My Levels of Power in the System

Power itself is not an issue; it is how it is used as discussed in the section above. Each of us has power and it can be helpful to contextualize levels of power within your school or workplace. All of us, regardless of our privileged or subordinated identities, have the potential to uphold or to disrupt harmful and oppressive practices and patterns, especially when we have been positioned to have authority over others within a hierarchical system. This realization can be uncomfortable.

Below is a chart with some ways to identify the level of power you hold within your organization. It may also be helpful to find or create an organizational chart for your setting to see how power is distributed.

Levels of Systemic Power

High Levels of Power/Influence	*Medium Levels of Power/Influence*	*Medium-Low Levels of Power/ Influence*	*Low Levels of Power/Influence*
Ability to formally reprimand others	Long-established relationships within the school and school community	Low seniority	Noncertified positions (e.g. custodial staff, transportation, nutritional services)
Ability to fire and hire others	High seniority within the school	One year or temporary contract	Younger students
Ability to be believed by other authority figures, including law enforcement	Union leader	Non-union member (because there is no union for the position or no union within the organization)	Students with societally marginalized identities
Long-established relationships within the school and school community	Union representation	Older students involved in student union or other committees that directly influence change	Families with societally marginalized identities
Peers/colleagues with same or similar social identities (likely to be believed and have influence over others)	Socially dominant identities	Societally marginalized identities	
Writes or approves policy changes	Families with dominant identities		
Selects new initiatives and/ or educational programs	Supervises others but does not have ability to hire or fire		
Supervises others			
Socially dominant identities			

Just as with social identities, you may have located yourself in different levels of power within your organization. Take a few minutes to respond to these prompts after reviewing the chart above:

- What is my level of power within my school/workplace?
- Who do I have the potential to have power over within the organizational hierarchy?

After completing your reflection, notice how your body and breath feel. Are you experiencing defensiveness? Overwhelm? Curiosity? Confusion? You don't need to do anything other than be with those emotions right now. If you are feeling overwhelmed revisit SOAR: *Soften, Observe, Acknowledge what is, Release judgment,* or TONAL: *Tune in, Observe sensations & thoughts, Name the emotion and experience, Allow the emotion to move, Loving response to self,* in order to move through your experiences.

Examining Two Leadership Styles

There are many leadership styles within education. We will unpack two general styles of leadership to compare and contrast. The first style is a form of *power over* leadership and the second is a form of *power with* leadership.

Power over leadership contributes to unhealthy school climates and cultures; it increases stress and burnout, and negatively impacts students and educators (Ahmed et al., 2024; Wolor et al., 2022). Toxic leadership is one form of using power over. This leadership approach seeks to control rather than collaborate and contributes to an unhealthy culture. Anastasiou (2025) outlines six traits of toxic leadership:

1. Authoritarian leadership: Excessive control over others, limiting creativity and autonomy.
2. Narcissism: Leaders with an inflated sense of self-importance, seeking personal gain.
3. Self-promotion: Prioritizing personal interests, avoiding responsibility and taking undue credit.

4. Unpredictability: Erratic moods create an unstable work environment.
5. Abusive supervision: Hostile behaviors like belittling or unfairly holding subordinates accountable.
6. Gender bias: Teachers may experience gender discrimination or sexual harassment by their school leadership.

While not mentioned, racial bias and other identity-based biases should also be included here. Educators of the Global Majority, disabled educators, LGBTQIA+ educators, and other educators whose identities are societally marginalized may also experience discrimination or harassment by those who utilize toxic leadership. This is vastly different from a power with leadership approach.

Power sharing, or *power with*, is the practice of sharing power across differences, expanding the power of a group by harnessing the diverse experiences, perspectives, and skills within the group, and ensuring that people within a system have opportunities to act (VeneKlasen & Miller, 2007). Transformative leadership is a *power with* form of leading.

Transformative leadership has been linked to increased overall educator well-being and job satisfaction (Menge & Gerick, 2026; Rizkie, 2022). There are many variations of transformative or transformational leadership. The six characteristics of transformative leadership below were synthesized from the work of Avant (2011), Dulfano (2018), Jun (2011), and Shields (2004):

1. Self-awareness. Actively reflects on their strengths and is willing to learn from missteps.
2. Open to change: Does not rely on "tradition" and is open to change in collaborative and power-balanced relationships with people within the school community.
3. Creates opportunities for genuine democratic participation and ensures that people within the school/school system who have been historically and presently underrepresented have access to opportunity for meaningful participation.

4. Addresses power imbalances and inequities:

   > transformative leaders need to spend some time taking an honest look at policies, programs, curriculum, and everyday practices in their schools in order to determine whether they are equitable and promote social justice. In addition, leaders need to look introspectively, to examine underlying beliefs that may not promote equity and justice.
   >
   > *(Jun, 2011, p. 239)*

5. Demonstrates empathy and care to people within the system.
6. Cultural competency: "knowledge of one's own culture as well as competencies to effectively interact across different cultures" (Avant, 2011, p. 119).

Sharing power is present in democratic leadership styles in which decision-making is a shared process. A school or workplace might have democratic decision-making in place, but some social identities within the organization and the community are perpetually overrepresented in those processes, as described earlier. It is not truly democratic if people with positional and identity-based power continue to be the ones who make decisions.

Reflecting on Leadership Styles in My Setting

Take some time to reflect on the leadership-style characteristics you observe within your setting. If you are a leader, take some time to reflect on how you tend to lead. None of this is to blame or shame anyone. Take note of the emotions that are surfacing and get curious toward them. Allow this an opportunity to be radically honest about the leadership style. Just as with beliefs and values, leadership styles are not fixed traits. If change is needed, change can occur. It is possible, and likely, that the leadership style you interact with, observe, or use crosses over between the two. For leaders, I strongly recommend seeking out honest (and perhaps anonymous) opinions from those you lead. Sometimes, we cannot see ourselves fully.

- What leadership characteristics do I observe in my school/workplace?
- What impact does this have on the climate and culture?
- What impact does it have on me? What emotions surface reflecting on this?
- What changes to my leadership style would be helpful?
- What emotions are present when I think about these changes?

Reflecting on Policies, Initiatives, and System Changes

Take some time to reflect on the who and the how of system change can support your analysis of how the three types of *over* operates within your school and/or your broader school system.

- Who is part of the change process?
- Who is not?
- Whose identities are overrepresented?
- Whose identities are underrepresented?
- What are the reasons people state for not including more varied perspectives in change processes?
- How many educational program changes have happened in the last three years?
- What turnover have you experienced in your school/school system?

Taking a historical view of the policy process is also important. As mentioned earlier, people in positions of power and with socially dominant identities often are creating policies, even though they are the least impacted.

- When were the policies first written?
- Who wrote them? Whose identities were represented? Whose were not?

- When were they updated?
- By whom? Whose identities were represented? Whose were not?
- What is the process to challenge and change policies?
- In what ways is the process inaccessible based on social identities?

After you complete this reflection, take note of how your body feels and the emotions that are surfacing.

Who Holds Power?

In education, there is a persistent belief that people at the top of a hierarchy are somehow "smarter, knowing more, being able to control and advise and fix" (Beyer, 2016, p. 37). This is an equity issue because, as Faolan Jones (2020) keenly noted, "People who hold dominant identities are over-represented in positions of power, influence and leadership. While people who hold marginalised identities are under-represented or completely excluded" (n.p.). We see this pattern in the composition of school boards.

There is overrepresentation of White people on school boards who influence and make decisions about policies and practices that impact students and families with whom they do not share social group membership (Ballotpedia, 2022; Pendharkar, 2022; Stephens, 2025). In the U.S., over 90% of school board members are White and more than 50% of the members identify as men (Ballotpedia, 2022; Stephens, 2025). According to Houston and Hartney of the Fordham Institute (2025), 35% of school board members have a four-year college degree compared to 21% of the U.S. public, and 46% of school board members have a post-graduate degree compared to 14% of the U.S. public (Houston & Hartney, 2025).

Overlaying the organizational hierarchy with race, gender, country of origin, and other identities is critical to truly understand the ways in which multiple oppressions are co-occurring within schools. These power-over conditions prevent schools from being trauma-informed or anti-oppressive.

Exploring the Organizational Hierarchy

1. Create an organizational hierarchy based on your setting.
    a. Discuss your draft hierarchy chart with other people, and revise.
    b. The certified educational staff
        i. Classroom teachers, including integrated arts
        ii. Special educators, school psychologists, behavior analysts, occupational therapists, physical therapists, speech language pathologists, guidance counselors, and other related professions.
    c. Non-certified educational staff
        iii. Para educators, interventionists, 1:1 support staff
        iv. Custodial staff
        v. Nutritional services
        vi. Transportation
    d. Administration
        vii. District level
        viii. Building level
    e. The student population
2. Layer in social identities on the hierarchy chart.

After you have created or co-created this chart, how would you describe the way power is distributed? Who holds power? What identities are overrepresented? What identities are underrepresented? This organizational chart can help you to identify who makes decisions and who does not.

Pause and Reflect

As you finish this chapter, take a moment to notice the thoughts and emotions that are surfacing for you. What level of overwhelm are you experiencing at the moment? What is your level of hopefulness? Do you feel energized? Remember, there is no "right" answer. These questions are simply here to help you better understand yourself and other people if you are working with a group. Take some time to process in a way that feels supportive through movement or rest.

Power Affirmations

- I do not need to wield power over others in order to effect change.
- Using *power over* does not lead us toward justice or healing.
- Addressing *power over* is necessary.
- Having power is not a problem; trying to use it to control others is.
- The use of *power over* contributes to burnout and moral injury.
- Sharing power with is far more potent than power over can ever be.

CHAPTER SUMMARY

The climate and culture of a school/school system is often hidden. Climate may feel "normal," but it may be contributing to a lack of wellness within the organization. When a climate or culture is organized around overwork, exhaustion, and pressure to perform perfectionism, and is combined with *power over* leadership approaches, the well-being of everyone within a school/school system suffers. It is necessary, and helpful, to understand how the use of power is either impeding progress toward equity and wellness or supporting it. These power imbalances create unhealthy work environments and can also maintain the status quo.

8

Identifying Bias in Our Schools

Implicit/Unconscious Biases

This chapter may bring up some strong emotions for you. As discussed in the previous chapters, continue to greet these emotions with curiosity, openness, and compassion. Your identities, lived experiences, and previous work connected to bias will all influence how you respond to this information. As discussed in the chapter on social identities, we have all been influenced by the messages we received about social identities in relation to power and privilege.

Implicit or unconscious biases are beliefs we hold about people and groups of people based on our socialization. These biases are manifestations of the ways we have been socialized and conditioned and they influence and shape our schools and school systems. Unconscious bias can lead to a "negative association of a group of community" and it can also lead to positive associations with a group or community (Agarwal, 2021, p. 13).

We must contend with the realities that: 1) we ourselves are biased; 2) these biases uphold the status quo in various ways; 3) no space we occupy is ever bias-free. One of the first steps of addressing injustices as they exist is to acknowledge that they *do* exist. It is critical that we constantly create space for ourselves to reflect on our biases, interrogate their origins, and then actively choose different patterns of thinking and action (Agarwal, 2021; Eberhardt, 2020; King, 2018; Magee, 2021).

DOI: 10.4324/9781003540687-9

But I Know Someone Who (insert societally marginalized identity here)...

Can we have relationships with people with whom we hold biases toward? Yes, and we must be persistent in disrupting the biased beliefs we hold all the time. Men have many relationships with women, and they are still biased against women. White teachers have relationships with Black and Brown youth and hold unconscious biases about them. Straight and cisgender people are friends with queer people and trans people and must still interrogate their homophobia and transphobia. Monoracial parents of mixed-race children can hold biased beliefs of their children. If we are not consciously interrupting our own unconscious beliefs and judgements about other people, it is impossible to be in an ethical relationship with people.

Reflecting on our Biases

Just as we did in the chapter on social identities, I invite you to write before you keep reading. Have you ever gone to the dentist, and when they ask you about your flossing habits, you tell them you floss daily, when, in fact, you haven't flossed since your last dentist visit? Or when you go to the doctor's office, and they ask you about your sleep hygiene, you tell them you get "at least 8 hours a night," but you haven't slept for more than 6 hours in years? This phenomenon is referred to as *social desirability bias* (Gower et al. 2022; Grant 2023). When we give someone an answer we think we will be socially acceptable, we are using *social desirability bias*. This may also prevent us from actively owning that we have biases.

Some people may subconsciously believe that if they admit to having biases, they are admitting to being a bad person. If this is you, I invite you to revisit the shame and shame-avoidance section. Acknowledging that you have biases is necessary in order to address them directly. We can't work with what we deny to be real. So, let's get real.

In Chapter 4, you reflected on your upbringing connected to having discussions (or not) about social identities. We are going to extend that reflection now. It may be helpful to practice one of the mindfulness practices, mini-practices, or any other form of grounding/centering practice that supports you in moving into a more relaxed and open state before you begin.

1. Using the chart of social identities, reflect on who you were taught (implicitly and explicitly through family, friends, school, media, etc.) to have positive and negative social bias toward (for media: think about the shows/ movies you watched growing up- who was represented and how and who was underrepresented).
2. How were certain groups of people represented? Positively? Negatively?
3. What were the stereotypes of groups?
4. What unconscious biases are revealing themselves through your process?
5. How might these unconscious biases show up in your interactions in schools/school systems?
6. What emotions came up for you as you reflected on your biases, their origins, and how they show up now?
7. In what ways do my biases and my identities prevent me from seeing the full picture of what is happening in our schools?

Pause & Reflect

As you wrote your responses, did anything surprise you? Our society steeps our hearts and minds with stories of who matters and who doesn't. Our families reinforced and/or disrupted these stories. Our experiences in schools reinforced and/or disrupted these stories.

Take a moment to acknowledge the work you just did. This is important. Even if this wasn't your first time, we need to be persistent in surfacing what is happening below our level of consciousness. We live in a society that encourages us to "move on" and to pretend that our histories don't matter. Compartmentalizing parts of us creates unnecessary fragmentation and doesn't allow us to tend to what needs to be healed for ourselves and our world.

Social Bias and Oppression Exist in Your School(s)

I often hear educators say "I love all of my students." It is a beautiful sentiment, but those words are not always reflected in actions. bell hooks (2001) wrote: "to truly love we must learn to mix various ingredients—care, affection, recognition, respect, commitment, and trust, as well as honest and open communication" (p. 5). Love is not pity. Love is not saviorism. Love is not believing that we are the only ones who can "fix" them. And love requires that we are *honest* with ourselves about how we treat people differently because of our biases. Pretending that there is racial or gender neutrality within your school/school system will only deepen the inequities and injustices that are already present.

Merriam-Webster (2025) defines oppression as: "unjust or cruel exercise of authority or power" (n.p.). There are many forms of oppression that all intersect and connect. All of their origins are found within power-over systems that:

> dictate that some peoples, nations, ethnicities, genders, and lives are more worthy of safety, belonging, dignity, and resources than others. Power-over declares that it is okay to leave many in poverty, hurt, and exploited, while we concentrate money, energy, power, and decision making over others and the commons to a very few. The social and economic distribution of dignity, safety, and belonging is how we construct who is seen as worthy of existing and who is considered expendable.
>
> *(Staci K. Haines, 2019, p. 55)*

These systems of power emerge in various ways.

For people with societally marginalized identities, it is often very apparent where and how these power-over systems exist (Magee, 2021; Sue, 2010, 2016). For people with dominant identities, it may be more challenging to identify the way they operate and exist. This statement is, of course, not universally true. Some people with socially dominant identities have dedicated time and energy to become much more aware of and disrupt social harms. The invisible form of *power over* described in the previous chapter and many social processes have insidiously worked to prevent people with societally marginalized identities from recognizing injustices.

Ideological, Institutional, Interpersonal, and Internalized Oppression

John Bell (2018a), a Buddhist Dharma teacher and social activist, offers a useful framework for understanding how social forms of oppression operate through the "Four I's:" Ideological, Institutional, Interpersonal, and Internalized. Bell emphasizes that these forms of oppression are interconnected and do not and cannot stand alone. In order to effectively disrupt oppression, all forms of oppression must be identified and addressed. We cannot selectively choose one to work on in hopes that the others will change without intentional focus. If you are working in education in the U.S., these forms of oppression have and continue to shape the system you are working in.

Ideological oppression is the basis for all of the other I's. It is the belief that a group or some groups are superior to, or better than, another group or other groups of people. The second "I" is *institutional oppression*. The ideologies of better than/less than become entrenched into the institutions within a society, such as schools, banks, medical care, and the policies that are built around ideological oppression. Institutional oppression is present in the "zero tolerance policies" that disproportionately harmed Black students who were pushed out of schools far more than their White counterparts (Bell, 2015; McCombs et al., 2022). The far-reaching impacts of being pushed out of school continue to disproportionately harm Black communities far more than other racial groups. These impacts are present in current immigration policies that target Black and Brown communities.

Interpersonal oppression is often the most noticed form of oppression, and many in-school trainings focus on this type of voppression. People with dominant identities will express the ideology that people with societally marginalized identities are lesser than through slurs, social exclusion, bullying, and harassment.

Internalized oppression is when people with societally marginalized identities believe they are lesser than. They may make self-loathing statements connected to their social group membership(s)/identities as "jokes." Bell (2018a) noted that "oppression always begins from outside the oppressed group, but by the time it gets internalized, the external oppression need hardly be felt for the damage to be done" (p. 4). In a YouTube video adaptation of the four I's of oppression, Elina Pipes (2016) reminds us that "it is never a person's fault" (n.p.) that they are experiencing internalized oppression. Within a society organized by social hierarchies, people with dominant identities may also internalize superiority (Sondel et al., 2019), believing, consciously or subconsciously, that they are better than people with societally marginalized identities.

Social Biases

Biases connected to social group membership are real and universal (Agarwal, 2021; Amemiya et al., 2020; Eberhardt, 2020; Sanchez & Bonam, 2009; Sue, 2010). We all have them. None of us are exempt from having to reflect on our biases and their impacts on our world. We have all been socialized to have bias. Unconscious biases operate below our level of awareness. We can disrupt these unconscious biases by: 1) knowing we have them; 2) naming them; and 3) actively challenging them.

Positive biases and negative biases connected to social group memberships/social identities come from cultural messaging from our upbringings within our families, important adults in our lives, and broader society (Agarwal, 2021; Bell, 2018b; Eberhardt, 2020; Harro, 2018). Positive social biases are when we ascribe positive attributes, qualities, and associations with certain groups of people. Examples of positive bias include: viewing men and boys as *natural* leaders (rational, authoritative, etc.) and placing them in leadership positions even though women (trans and cis), genderqueer, and nonbinary people are equally or more qualified; or viewing people with college degrees as *smarter* or *more successful*. Agarwal (2021) reminds us that when a "positive bias creates a negative discrimination against someone else or if it gives someone an undue advantage to the favoured group over someone else, then it becomes problematic" (p. 12).

Negative biases ascribe negative attributes, qualities, and associations with certain groups of people. Examples of negative bias include: viewing people experiencing poverty as *unmotivated, lazy* and *unwell*, rather than critiquing our society and the ways it creates and perpetuates poverty and generational poverty; or assuming women are more *emotional* and therefore *irrational* and not believing them or discrediting their knowledge and lived experiences.

Public schools are not safe havens where all students find comfort, ease, and their whole selves honored (Annamma, 2018; Ighodaro & Wiggan, 2009; Love, 2019; Morris, 2016; Venet, 2021). This truth is particularly salient for students of the Global Majority, disabled students, multicultural, multilingual, LGBTQIA+ students, and students whose identities span across those social identities (e.g. Black disabled students experience schools far differently than their White disabled peers; Annamma, 2018; Annamma et al., 2016). Resmaa Menakem (2017) wrote:

> Everyone, no matter what their skin color, experiences such minor violations occasionally. When they occur only now and then, they are easy enough to shrug off as tolerable, then heal from and forget. But when these violations happen repeatedly (whether over months for an individual or centuries for a group), in many different situations and with many different people over time, they create [a] toxic hazy trauma.
>
> *(p. 77)*

The persistent belief that trauma is something that happens to "those kids" and occurs "out there" prevents schools from addressing the trauma occurring within schools. As people working in education, we need to address the identity-based trauma that occurs in schools (Butts 2002; Duane 2023; Gaffney 2019; Saleem et al. 2020).

Challenging Our Assumptions

During one of my visits to a preschool classroom during snack, I made my way around the tables and said hello to students. When I asked one student about her snack, she looked up at me with her brow furrowed and eyes narrowed and said "Don't talk to me, I don't know you!" Before I tell how I responded, and how the other educators in the room responded, I want to pause and invite you to take a moment to reflect on how *you* would react in this scenario. Not what you think you *should* say, but what immediate visceral response would you have? What immediate visceral response *did* you have reading that? What would you say to this child? How are you imagining this child racially?

She was a young Black girl. This matters because Black girls are overrepresented in the school-to-prison pipeline. Black girls are more frequently believed to be *disrespectful*, *defiant*, and *adult-like* (Annamma 2018; Gilliam, et al., 2016; Morris 2016). She was in a classroom of mostly White students with White classroom teachers. Now I'll tell you how I responded.

My immediate emotional reaction was a sense of surprise. I am sure my eyes widened and I probably did a slow blink. I am so used to young children being responsive to adults, and I pride myself on being someone who gets along well with young children. It took a second for my surprise to turn into warmth. I smiled and responded, "You're right; you don't," and I slowly walked away and continued to move around the classroom. I posted this interaction on social media and have shared this same scenario in workshops I have given. The responses are widely varied.

Some people were so proud and impressed that this young Black girl was so clear in naming her boundaries and reflected that she must have some great adult role models. Other people shared discomfort with a child being "disrespectful" to an adult. A group of Native Hawaiian educators talked about the expectations within their own culture and that community members are expected to be warm and inviting to everyone. This very small moment points to the importance of unpacking our own cultural shaping and to disrupt any belief that there is some universal "norm".

I am certain that the young Black preschooler who set a firm and healthy boundary with a stranger (me) will at far too many points in her academic career, and in the world more broadly, be told that she is being "rude," "disrespectful," and needs to "tone it down." Had this particular preschool team not gone through extensive anti-bias training, I can guarantee that the student would have received a response of, "Well, that's not nice. We need to be nice to people when they're nice to us. Say sorry." I guarantee that because that is what I have observed time and time again.

Himpathy in Schools

In this next section, we will be exploring gender-based violence. If this topic is too personal, please take time away from this content.

Kate Manne (2020) coined the term *himpathy* to explain the ways that in our patriarchal society, men are frequently given more empathy and compassion compared to other genders. *Himpathy* is an example of positive social bias. The more socially dominant identities a person holds, the more likely they are to receive *himpathy* (e.g. Cisgender, White, Heterosexual, Man). When cisgender boys and men are asked to be accountable for sexist, racist, and/or queerphobic words and/or actions, people will find ways to explain away the behavior.

Himpathy is present in our schools every day. The data continue to show that girls and LGBTQIA+ students are significantly more likely to experience sexual violence and that perpetrators of that violence are almost always cisgender boys or men (Valenti and Friedman 2020). Cisgender boys and men benefit from the positive bias of being believed at the expense of the people who have been harmed by their actions. *Himpathy* also prevents cisgender boys and men from engaging in the healing work that is only possible through taking responsibility for harm done to others.

In classrooms, these patterns manifest in a multitude of ways. White boys from financially privileged backgrounds who act rambunctious may be labeled as "class clowns" and rarely receive reprimand, while Black students and poor White students who engage in identical or nearly identical behaviors are labeled as "troublemakers" and are disproportionately represented in special education and in disciplinary consequences (Annamma, 2018; Fadus et al., 2020; National Prevention Science Coalition, 2020; Voulgarides et al., 2017). When we punish and exclude girls, BIPOC students, disabled students, queer, and trans students, we show them they are unworthy, and we simultaneously teach students with dominant identities that they, too, have a right to enact this type of punishment and exclusion.

Identifying Bias in the System

The racial, ethnic, linguistic, and cultural diversity in U.S. schools continues to increase, and with this increase in diversity, ample opportunities arise to challenge mindsets and expectations for what is "normal" and "expected" behavior. The data continue to show us that Black students, poor students, and students of the Global Majority continue to be overrepresented nationally in disciplinary referrals and underrepresented nationally in traditionally White upper-class spaces, such as advanced placement courses. In the U.S., 80% of the public educator workforce is White, compared to the student population, which is 46% White (Kent 2024).

Research indicates that we are most likely to have positive biases with those most similar to us, and we will, therefore, feel more empathy and take action that reflects care (Eberhardt, 2020). If you are a White educator, reflect on how this shapes your relationships with students of the global majority. This may show up as insisting that White students receive support and ensuring access to services and supports, while Black and Brown families and students are perceived as less deserving. The White family and Black or Brown family may have nearly identical situations in terms of need, but it is the White family and students who receive support and care. This is not to say that White families and students do not deserve care, but we need to increase awareness and take honest assessments of which students and families are more likely to receive culturally-connected supports. This reflection is essential in disrupting the persistent imbalance and injustice of access to culturally-sustaining education and services (Dhaliwal, 2016; Howard et al., 2020; Ladson-Billings, 2021).

Implicit or unconscious biases can manifest as hidden social rules viewed as "the norm," but which are upholding various forms of oppression. We interpret student behavior based on our biases. *Confirmation bias* is when we find exactly what we are looking for, regardless of counterevidence. In the previous chapter about *burnout, moral injury*, and *secondary trauma response*, we made the connection that when our nervous systems are overwhelmed, we are more likely to rely on confirmation bias. This is a problem.

One example of confirmation bias is when educators search for a diagnosis to explain why a student isn't thriving in school. Once an educator believes that the root cause is ADHD or autism, they are constantly looking for signs of "proof," but they are not looking for alternative explanations.

An educator may be hyper-focused on that one particular child and searching for proof (confirmation bias) without zooming out and seeing that nearly 30% of the students in the room are fidgeting, staring at the ceiling, or putting their heads on the table at any given moment. The students that are frequently subjected to this *hyper-surveillance, hyper-labeling*, and then *hyper-punishment* (Annamma, 2018) are frequently students of color, particularly Black students, multilingual, poor, and/or gender-nonconforming (Amemiya et al., 2020; Bal et al., 2014; National Prevention Science Coalition, 2020; Voulgarides et al., 2017).

If we are consistently ascribing negative qualities to Black students, poor students, multilingual students, queer students, and other students whose identities have been historically and presently devalued in the dominant society, through our actions, inactions, curriculum, interactions, and biased beliefs, not only are those students being harmed, but we are also modeling how students from dominant groups should perceive and interact with their peers. When some students are held to higher and different standards than others, unconscious bias presents itself and reinforces beliefs entrenched in our society. Displays of these unconscious biases further the beliefs that some students are worthy of care, patience, and are skilled, while others are devalued and dehumanized. Your students are observing your actions, taking note, internalizing them, and replicating them. Below are some examples of unconscious biases and how their impacts ripple outward:

- *A boys' swim team poses shirtless for the yearbook. In the same school, there is a dress code that has sent multiple young women and girls home (mostly Black and economically disadvantaged) for wearing outfits that are too "revealing." This same school disallows trans youth from participating on teams with their cisgender peer counterparts.*
- *LGBTQIA+ youth advocate for firmer anti-discrimination and anti-bullying practices that hold their non-LGBTQIA+ peers and educators accountable for harm they cause. They outline the ways the current policies are not being enforced and make suggestions on how policies and practices can be modified. They are told that there is a process for policy change and that it's a really "complicated issue." They are told that they will need to practice more self-advocacy in the meantime and to "just stand up for themselves."*
- *Players on sports teams are given passes for assignments and have absences excused. Students with chronic health conditions are required to get doctor's notes to prove their discomfort is real and their absences or reduced workload are valid.*
- *Middle- and upper-class students and families are underrepresented in Department of Children and Families (DCF) reports.*
- *Disabled and neurodivergent students are prevented from accessing the mobility, sensory, and communication supports they need in order to thrive.*

The impact of unconscious biases, as they play out in our schools, is not just caused by the biases outside of school walls; schools are replicating them. For example, in Pragya Agarwal's (2021) book *Unravelling Unconscious Bias*, she noted that

> Research in education shows that wrong answers provided by boys are more likely to be overlooked. In contrast, girls are more often criticized for incorrect answers, and teachers tend to provide them with less praise for correct answers. An unconscious bias therefore develops that boys' knowledge is more highly valued than girls', which can convince girls they are less competent than boys.
>
> *(p. 10)*

This bias results in all genders unconsciously believing that the knowledge of anyone who is not a "boy" or a "man" is less valuable. This messaging also encourages boys who become adult men to believe they are right; they will struggle inwardly and outwardly when they are challenged by others.

One of the most frequent pitfalls people share is that there aren't enough data to identify bias within the school or school system. I always find this puzzling. Educators are tasked with collecting an unfathomable amount of data: both educational and behavioral data. One issue is that there might be too much data or the wrong kind of data to address the issues. Talking around a problem never actually addresses it. If it seems that the data available aren't adequate in your setting, there is always a path to get started: a) use the data you do have, and b) work collaboratively to identify what data you have, what data are redundant, and what data is needed in order to create change. Schools are often encouraged to be over-reliant on standardized assessment, and while these data reveal some information, they are missing the heart-data; the lived realities and stories of people.

Data Analysis Warm-Up

In every school, there are common stories about data. The stories are work-arounds to avoid addressing the issues. Take some time to reflect on these prompts:

1. In your school/school system, what are the stories that people share when faced with data that show disparities between groups of students?
2. Have these stories changed over the years?
3. Has the data changed?
4. Who in the system is responsible for the outcomes presented in the data?
5. What impact might *burnout* and *secondary trauma responses* have on people when trying to address disparities?

Gathering Data and Telling New Stories

Revisit *Who Holds Power* from Chapter 7, prior to reviewing the following prompts.

1. Look at the Youth Risk Behavior Survey (YRBS) data or comparable data for your school/system.
   a. Which students are being actively harmed?
   b. What social identities are overrepresented in different categories?
   c. What have been some biased explanations about this data?
2. Which students are overrepresented in school disciplinary responses?
3. Which students are overrepresented in special education referrals and/or identification?
4. Which students are underrepresented in special education referrals and/or identification?
5. Which students are overrepresented in extracurricular activities?
6. Which students are underrepresented in extracurricular activities?
7. Which student groups are overrepresented in meeting educational standards?
8. Which student groups are overrepresented in *not* receiving in or out of schools suspensions or other behavioral referrals (i.e. office visit referrals)?
9. Has the data significantly changed over the past few years?
   a. Is there evidence of disproportionality?
10. Who do you believe is responsible for the data being the way they are?
11. How can we make sense of this data through the 4 I's of oppression framework?

Educators of the Global Majority, queer, trans, multiracial, multilingual educators, and any educator whose identity is societally marginalized, are also unlikely to believe that schools are neutral or haven-like (Lisle-Johnson & Kohli, 2020; Shah & Grimaldos, 2022). Below are additional examples of how social identities/social group memberships impact who is given access and how people are treated:

- White educators are given awards and public recognition for diversity, equity, and inclusion efforts (e.g., highly visible and visually aesthetic posters, events, etc.), while educators of the Global Majority are often tone-policed for initiating justice-centered change (e.g., naming that there is racism happening and making suggestions for policy and practice change).
- Disabled educators are underrepresented. Hiring practices and procedures, as well as other systemic barriers, prevent equitable access for disabled educators to be in the field.
- LGBTQIA+ educators are underrepresented and/or are infrequently not *out* because of fear of homophobic/queerphobic/transphobic backlash and harm.

Reflecting on Bias in Family-School Relationships

Similarly, parents of the Global Majority and from other subordinated/societally marginalized identities are also unlikely to feel like they are truly part of the school community or that their needs are centered (Shah & Grimaldos, 2022). Reflect on this at both the personal level and the systemic level: how do *your* biases play out here? And what trends do you notice across your educational setting?

- Which families' requests are heard and honored?
- Which families' requests are ignored and actively marginalized?
- Which families are spoken about with warmth?
- Which families are spoken about with judgment?
- Which families are more likely to be reported to Child Protective Services?
- What patterns are you noticing?
- How does this feel in your body?
- What emotions are surfacing?

Identifying and Addressing Intention–Action Gaps

In schools, where the norms have been organized around sameness and notions of normalcy based in White, middle-class, college-educated values (Love 2019; Knaus 2018; Shah and Grimaldos 2022), there needs to be a persistent effort to uproot those false notions of normalcy and co-create something better for everyone. bell hooks (2001) offered us this way of learning how to be in community with other people:

> Cultures of domination rely on the cultivation of fear as a way to ensure obedience. In our society we make much of love and say little about fear. Yet we are all terribly afraid most of the time. As a culture, we are obsessed with the notion of safety. Yet we do not question why we live in states of extreme anxiety and dread. Fear is the primary force upholding systems of domination. It promotes the desire for separation, the desire not to be known. When we are taught that safety always lies in sameness, then difference, of any kind, will appear as a threat. When we choose to love we choose to move against fear – against alienation and separation. The choice to love is the choice to connect – to find ourselves in the other
>
> *(p. 93)*

bell hooks (2000) wrote that "to be truly visionary we have to root our imagination in our concrete reality while simultaneously imagining possibilities beyond that reality" (p. 110). When we disrupt biases in our schools and school systems, we are not just addressing oppression, we are changing the trajectory of the future.

Pause and Reflect

Take some time to reflect on how your body, heart, and mind are feeling as you finish this chapter. If it is helpful and there is time, use one of the foundational or mini-mindfulness practices before reflection. Then revisit your values reflection from Chapter 5, where you identified personal intention–action gaps. After you revisit those, reflect on these questions:

- Are we truly reaching all students?
- Are we truly reaching all families?

- Are staff all treated equitably?
- Who is receiving care in our system?
- Who is receiving the message that they don't belong?
- What do we need in order to cultivate school cultures that organize around compassion, mutual respect, safety, and belonging?
- How can we address our individual biases and systemic barriers to better support students? Each other? Families?

Take some time to process your reflection in a way that feels supportive through movement or rest.

Addressing Bias Affirmations

- ♦ Biases are everywhere in our society and our schools. The more we accept that, the more we can address them.
- ♦ Having biases doesn't make me a bad person, but I am responsible for how those biases impact other people.
- ♦ I am capable of addressing and changing my biased beliefs.

CHAPTER SUMMARY

We all have positive and negative social biases. Our unconscious beliefs about people we work with and about students we serve impact everyone in the system. People with socially dominant identities continue to experience more positive messages about their identities and people with societally marginalized identities endure numerous examples of identity-based harm in schools. Examining our data, even if it is imperfect, and using the data to identify biased decision-making is necessary in order to address and disrupt these patterns and practices.

9

The Impact of Biased Perceptions of Emotions

Biased Perceptions of Emotional Expression

Our socialization and our biases influence how we teach and connect with our colleagues and with youth. In many school cultures organized around White middle-class values, there is a pervasive idea that there are "normal" and "abnormal" ways to express emotions. This can be seen in "the well-established bias of the behavioral expectations of children who do not conform, or as seen by authority as unable or unwilling to conform, experience negative outcomes. These overwhelmingly are students of color or of low SES" (Knestrict, 2018, p. 84). These expectations also are present in our interactions with adults, including our colleagues and families.

Emotional expression is not universal. Someone may feel anger and get very still and very quiet, while someone else might increase the volume of their voice and move around. They are both feeling anger but they are showing it differently. There are also cultural differences in when, how, and with whom anger is expressed (Linklater, 2014; Yoo & Chung, 2010). A family may experience frustration with an educator but hesitate to share their frustration because of their cultural expectations that educators should not be questioned by families. Other families, often with socially dominant identities, express their frustration with educators and education without hesitation. Depending on their level of power and

DOI: 10.4324/9781003540687-10

influence (e.g. White, wealthy, involved in the community or on the school board), that frustration will be addressed while other families' concerns go unnoticed and/or not responded to.

Reflection

Before you continue reading, take a moment to surface some subconscious beliefs. Read through this list. Write or say aloud the first person who comes to mind as you read each characteristic. It can be people you know or fictional characters. Do not overthink this; let your subconscious mind do the work for you.

Charismatic	Passionate	Thoughtful
Courageous	Decisive	Naive
Calm	Formidable	Natural Leader
Warm	Melodramatic	Innocent
Spunky	Attention-seeking	Gentle
Generous	Genius	Combative
Loving	Sweet	Aggressive
Gentle	Compassionate	Spontaneous
Sweet	Patient	Adventurous
Helpless		

What did you notice about who came to mind for the different characteristics? Were your responses gendered? Racialized? Ability-based? How do you *feel* about your responses? Were you surprised?

Each time we make the effort to surface our socialization, we choose to disrupt our biased beliefs and the ways those biases influence our world.

Expressions of emotions are inherently complex. Social identities influence how people's emotions are perceived and create a bind for everyone. All people experience emotions, but there is different social conditioning to express or repress emotional experiences to fit in; to not be regarded as threatening; and to feel emotionally, psychologically, and physically safe. Emotions are not gendered, but expectations of emotional experience and expression are gendered (Barrett 2017).

Socially-Created Emotional Expectations

Within a U.S. context, White men in positions of power are often afforded opportunities to express anger and indignation. As boys, they were socialized and raised to believe that in order to fit into the gender role of "boy" or "man," they needed to be competitive, express anger, be invulnerable, confident, and take risks. There is societal pressure for men to be decision-focused, logical, and stoic, and there is a lack of encouragement for them to practice empathy, compassion, and collaboration (Chamorro-Premuzic 2019; Chemaly 2018; Hackman 2023; Valenti & Friedman 2020; hooks 2004; Nagoski & Nagoski 2020). These pressures are detrimental to everyone's well-being.

Boys are taught that they must be strong, infallible, emotionally stoic, competitive, and receivers of care (Hackman, 2023; hooks, 2004; Nagoski & Nagoski, 2020; Samaran, 2019). To counter this, we need to first examine the ways boys are conditioned to enact these rigid gender roles, and then we need to actively support young boys to navigate being fallible, making mistakes, expressing care, and collaborating with others. When we habitually put boys and young men into leadership positions or praise them for being confident and competitive, we are showing them and everyone else in those classrooms who is worthy of leadership and who is not. These boys and young men become adult men who then have had a lifetime of experience suppressing their emotional range, believing they are entitled to as much airtime as they would like, and expecting others to be responsible for their emotional well-being.

Reflecting on Our Emotional Socialization

It may be helpful to revisit one of the mindfulness practices from either chapter one or chapter two. You can also use any other form of grounding/centering practice that supports you in moving into a more relaxed and open state. Then revisit the social group membership chart and the emotion chart.

- In your upbringing, how did your social identities influence the ways you were taught about emotions and emotional expression?
- Who modeled emotional expression or emotional repression in your youth?

- Which emotions were socially acceptable and which ones were not?
- How do you see that shaping how you interact with your own emotions and the emotions of others?

Biased Emotional Perceptions

Our biases are present when someone is expressing their emotions. As mentioned in Chapter 8, our biases are operating all the time. It takes conscious effort to surface these mental shortcuts so that we are not acting on biased beliefs. Interrogating our biases, and our comfort and discomfort with emotions and displays of certain emotions, is essential in creating educational spaces and relationships with others that are humanizing and liberatory.

In *My Grandmother's Hands*, Resmma Menakem (2017) explores the ways in which White people have been socialized to fear Black people. That fear can result in hypersurveillance and hyperpunishment of Black people, in particular (Annamma 2018), and also of other societally marginalized people. In a 2016 study, researchers at the Yale University Child Study Center asked both White and Black preschool educators to identify misbehavior while watching a small group of Black and White children in a preschool setting. All educators overidentified the Black students, particularly the Black preschool boys, as having "misbehavior." There was no misbehavior happening. This has far-reaching consequences.

For example, if a Black student, who is called a slur by a smiling White student in the hallway, reacts with any form of warranted outrage, they are more likely to face disciplinary consequences for their warranted response than their White peer counterpart. Our Black youth may stifle their justified anger so they are not punished. This emotional stifling can wreak havoc on overall health and well-being. We need to address our biased beliefs and create spaces where students have opportunities to fully express themselves when harm is caused by racial or other identity-based oppression. The White peer who was actually misbehaving faces no consequences and does not have the opportunity to experience healthy guilt, remorse, regret, and humility.

Emotional suppression for people who experience social harm, based on their race, gender identity, sexual orientation, disability, and documentation status, is particularly damaging. Not only do we first experience social harm, we may need to silence our reasonable emotional response in order to prevent further social harm. This is particularly true when it comes to expressions of anger.

The Social Rules of Anger

Anger on the outside can appear the same. However, our interpretations of anger are highly dependent on *who* is expressing anger. Black women, in particular, are under immense pressure to not seem "too angry" or "combative," even when addressing anger-inducing situations, like racism and sexism, and women and femmes across racial and ethnic backgrounds are almost immediately discounted and discredited if they express anything other than stereotypical "feminine" traits (Chemaly, 2018; Hackman, 2023; Leiba, 2022; Valenti & Friedman, 2020). When women and femmes deviate from rules, such as being patient, understanding, soft, empathetic, and compassionate, they are often met with punishment and rejection (Hackman, 2023). Girls and women, and gender-nonconforming people, especially people of the Global Majority/People of Color, express anger or frustration that they are deemed as being untrustworthy, hysterical, and dangerous (Hackman, 2023; Sieghart 2022; Sue 2010; Valenti & Friedman 2020). This is in direct opposition to societal rules that allow more grace for White men to express anger and to be believed (Manne, 2020).

Displaying competitiveness, aggressiveness, confidence, or anger by people who do not present as cisgender White boys/men is often met with social rejection or social punishment. There are some exceptions (e.g. playing sports); in general, however, these are the social rules of emotion playing out in the broader society.

bell hooks (2010) reminded us that "patriarchy has no gender" (p. 70). This means all of us have the responsibility to identify and disrupt the racialized and gendered rules within a patriarchal system. Women and femmes may have internalized the belief that women and femmes should be soft, gentle, and patient, even when being treated inequitably. People of all genders can and do uphold patriarchy.

There is a cost to preventing young boys and men from learning cooperation and compassion for them and for our society. We need boys and men to unlearn the rigid rules of patriarchy that teach them their worth is connected to competition (winning and being superior to others), receiving care from others (especially women and girls), and not demonstrating care or compassion to others (hooks 2004; Chamorro-Premuzic 2019; Quartana and Burns 2010). Encouraging people of all genders to have complete access to the full range of emotions available to us without fear of social rejection or punishment is one of the many ways we create schools that are justice centered and sites of healing. It may be helpful to revisit one of the mindfulness practices from either chapter one or chapter two. You can also use any other form of grounding/centering practice that supports you in moving into a more relaxed and open state then reflect on the questions below.

Reflecting on Emotional Expression in Your Setting

- What emotions are discouraged broadly in your setting?
- What emotions are freely expressed by which social identities?
  - (e.g. are girls, queer, and trans students encouraged to show empathy, patience and compassion while cis boys are encouraged to be "class clowns" and competitive?)
  - What are some of the impacts of this emotional socialization?
- What would you like to challenge in your own work with youth and/or adults?
- What is in your power to change?
- Who needs to be part of these conversations?
- Are the practices and methods of teaching emotional skills we are using creating safety or sameness?

The Impact of Bias on Educators in Your Organization

When underrepresented people do not conform to standard operating modes or attempt to bring attention to the ways in which systems of oppression are harming them and other people, they go from "pet-to-threat" and may experience "increased hostility, suspicion, isolation" from colleagues and supervisors and may also feel "disoriented and disillusioned by being confronted with even greater suspicion, distrust, and alienation from colleagues" (Thomas et al., 2013, p. 277). People whose identities have been societally marginalized and are underrepresented in the educational workforce, may find that they are "career pioneers who find themselves as solos in their workplace" (Thomas et al., 2013, p. 276). Thomas and colleagues (2016) define "pet" as "professional employees who are members of underrepresented groups may be welcomed into their workplaces, yet may be embraced for all of the wrong reasons. A pet is beloved, cared for, and often treated in a child-like fashion" (p. 276). This experience may also be true for students with societally marginalized identities who are in Advanced Placement (AP) classes and other spaces from which they have been historically excluded.

Schools and other organizations often want to increase the racial diversity of their educational staff. However, without examining the experiences of existing educators with marginalized identities in your organization, hiring more "diverse" educators will do nothing to ensure retention and/or a psychologically and physically safe working environment.

In my experience, the people who bring issues to the surface about systemic inequities and problematic policies are often tone-policed, silenced, and reprimanded; they are never the ones who receive public praise. These people are often, but not always, people whose identities have been societally marginalized. Conversely, usually people with positional power and/or privileged identities receive credit for ideas that were not theirs.

Story

In a meeting on a team that meets biweekly to discuss student behavior, Xiomara, an Afro-Latina, bilingual paraprofessional, surfaces an observation she has been making over the past couple of years. The rest of the team is White. There is one White man named Mark, who did a year of study abroad in college in Santiago, Chile. He is married to a Chilean woman and he is fluent in Spanish. The rest of the team is monolingual and all speak English.

Xiomara says she notices some students who are also bilingual and multilingual actively rejecting or avoiding speaking their home language(s) at school. She has tried speaking Spanish with some Spanish-speaking students, but they seem embarrassed and sometimes ignore her, ask her why she's speaking Spanish, or respond to her in English. She also notices this happening with student peers who also speak Spanish. She openly shares her experiences of growing up bilingual and the fear she felt speaking Spanish with peers or with Spanish-speaking teachers at school. She suggests starting a multilingual club and asks if other people have ideas of how to integrate multiple languages throughout the school.

In response, there were some head nods and some comments of "Wow, I'm so sorry that happened to you" and "Well, at least things are different now." Mark, who speaks Spanish, doesn't say anything during this meeting. Later, he meets with the principal, a White woman, and he talks about his Chilean wife and tells her he is fluent in Spanish. He pitches the idea of starting a Spanish club after school that he and his wife would run.

At the next meeting, the principal tells the team that Mark and his wife Luciana will be starting a Spanish-speaking club after school. The team congratulates Mark and tells him what a great idea that will be. There is an article written in the local newspaper with a picture of Mark and his wife and a description of the club they are starting. No one acknowledges Xiomara's original idea of a multilingual club has been taken over by a White man.

This is not the first time that Xiomara has had her ideas ignored and/or has had a White colleague take them and be given credit. She has, on more than one occasion, brought this up to her direct supervisor, a Chinese American special educator, Chloe, and to her principal. Her direct supervisor has had similar experiences and is equally frustrated. Xiomara, Chloe, and the principal have a meeting, which results in both Xiomara and Chloe feeling disheartened. The principal's messages in the meetings included: "We're a team!" and "We are always using each other's ideas. We can't always credit everyone who is involved."

After this more egregious example of her words and ideas simultaneously being dismissed then being championed by a

White educator, in addition to the frequent sense of isolation of being one of two Black educators and frequent microaggressions, Xiomara begins to search for a new job and leaves the school before the end of the year. Chloe also realizes how challenging it is to work in this environment and also starts a job search.

It is often easier to perceive other people's flaws and the ways they are upholding organizational dysfunction than it is to recognize our contributions to dysfunction. Perhaps your ideas haven't been taken and re-pitched, but maybe you've witnessed this happening, felt stuck, and said nothing. Maybe you've been the principal and focused on being a "team," while perpetuating the erasure of the contributions of educators whose identities are societally marginalized. You likely have witnessed something similar to the above example, perhaps to a less obvious degree, and didn't realize at the time that it was a symptom of broad systemic issues.

Pause & Reflect

- In this example, what did you *feel?*
- Who did you find yourself empathizing with?
- Who have you been in similar scenarios; which role(s) did you play?

In the above example, or similar scenarios you have been witness to or impacted by, someone may try to maneuver around the harm that Xiomara endured by focusing on the fact that Mark is generally a good guy, well-liked, and would never "do anything to intentionally hurt anyone." Mark is probably a good guy and well-liked and his actions erased the contributions of his Black colleague. Both of these can be true at the same time. As discussed in the previous chapter, Mark is receiving *himpathy* at Xiomara's expense.

Disrupting Biased Emotional Perceptions with Empathy

We all need empathy and we all deserve to have our stories, experiences, and perspectives fully heard. Your empathetic capacity is dependent on your abilities to notice, name, and navigate your own emotions. For example, if you are uncomfortable or avoidant of your own anxiety, it might be challenging to be with other people whose anxiousness expresses itself in ways you struggle with yourself and/or were taught were unacceptable ways of experiencing anxiety. Our own relationship with our emotions influences and impacts our relationship to other people's emotions.

In a course I taught, students paired up and practiced deep listening. The prompt was to share a story about their favorite food and what they liked about that food. The listener's only job was to listen without responding. During the whole-group reflection, one of the listeners noted that they really hated the food their partner talked about loving. They reflected that it was interesting to simultaneously feel their own disgust and their listening partner's joy and happiness. That is exactly what empathy is. We do not need to have emotional sameness; we are creating room for their emotions and our emotions to exist simultaneously even if they are incongruent.

There are so many ways in which we cannot fully understand someone else's world. At times, that can create discomfort and uneasiness within us. Revisit your social group membership work. The identities you hold can influence how receptive you are to other peoples lived experiences. Sometimes we negate people's experiences because we haven't experienced ourselves. We may subconsciously or consciously tell ourselves that if we don't understand it, then it must not be true.

Here are some examples: a) a non-disabled person who has never used assistive devices feels resistant and irritated by how long it is taking to make spaces physically accessible; b) a hearing person may not understand the importance of a classroom wide sound amplification system and doesn't want to be bothered with it; c) a cisgender person may scoff at and disbelieve the exclusionary experiences a trans person endures daily; d) a White person misinterprets the experiences of a person of the Global Majority with racism as exaggerations; and e) A monoracial person who has never experienced monoracism (the denial of a mixed-race person's experience) dismisses a mixed-race person's experience as being "not that bad". In order to build understanding we must strengthen our capacity of deep empathy.

Empathy doesn't mean being in someone else's shoes. Empathy is seeing the shoes someone is wearing and believing their story about how they are experiencing those shoes. Empathy creates room for us to be experiencing an uncomfortable feeling *with* someone else. We don't need to have lived through someone else's life (or worn their shoes) to be empathetic and believe someone.

Communicating Understanding with Empathy

Theresa Wiseman (Wiseman, 1996) identified four components of empathy: taking on someone's perspective; being non-judgmental; recognizing someone else's emotion or understanding their feelings; and communicating your understanding of a person's feelings. The chart below is adapted from Wiseman's work.

Four Elements of Empathy (adapted from Wiseman,1996)

Perspective: Take someone's perspective as their truth. Be willing to understand their story and perspective of events. You may not agree but you are willing to recognize their truth as their truth.	**Recognize and Disrupt Internal Judgment**: Notice your own patterns of judgment, bias, and assumptions. Label them as they show up and then invite them to take a rest.
Recognize and Understand the Person's Emotions/Feelings: Experience another person's feelings with them. Notice the difference between their feelings and your feelings in response to their feelings.	**Communicate Your Understanding of Their Feelings**: Acknowledge their feelings and validate that their feelings make sense, are legitimate, and reasonable.

Perspective

Taking someone else's perspective can be challenging. I have heard White educators express that it is challenging for them to "step into the shoes of someone else" because they have never lived as a Person of the Global Majority. I have never heard that sentiment from People of the Global Majority. We can all build our empathetic capacity. For people with socially dominant identities, this does not mean seeking out people with societally marginalized identities and asking them to share their experiences with you. You must first build meaningful friendships not transactional ones. When there is relational trust, those experiences will be part of your conversations. Relational trust is built with empathy not extraction.

You can also increase your empathetic capacity by reading more fiction (Bal & Veltkamp, 2013) written by and about people with societally marginalized identities. A practice I have committed to over the years is to read as many fictional and non-fictional stories of people whose identities are different from mine. I do not need to actually "walk a mile in someone else's shoes" in order to believe them when they tell me what that mile felt like for them.

It can be very tempting to want to correct someone's perspective of events. However, when we are settling into an empathetic mode, we must work on settling into a state of observation and curiosity rather than "fix it" mode. SOAR: *Soften, Observe, Acknowledge what is, Release judgment*, can be helpful in moving into this state. This doesn't mean we don't come back to a part of someone's story later that perhaps had something worth revisiting—especially if something they shared was racist, sexist, transphobic, classist, ableist, etc. It just means that in this particular moment, we are listening with curiosity and openness.

Recognize and Disrupt Internal Judgment

As noted in Chapter 2, the more we can recognize our judgments as they are happening the easier they are to release. A gentle internal note to ourselves might sound like "Oh, I'm judging that right now" or any other phrase that is authentic to you can be helpful.

Recognize and Understand the Person's Emotions/Feelings

This is where our own emotional granularity really supports us in being able to tune into the emotional world of someone else. When someone is sharing a story with us we may also feel feelings that are not actually being felt by the person telling us the story. They might be sad but we might feel uncomfortable with sadness. When we are more attuned to our own emotions, we can separate out what is ours and what is theirs and hold space for both. Learning how to sit in discomfort with ourselves creates more capacity for us to sit in discomfort with others.

Communicate Your Understanding of Their Feelings

This can be tricky, especially if we are feeling judgy or we want to correct or adjust someone's story. It can be even more challenging if we feel like we are being blamed or called out. Checking in on our nervous system state and our emotional responses when someone else is sharing their experience is necessary for empathetic responses. The practice of setting aside our wants and needs in the moment and validating someone else is incredibly powerful for the person receiving the empathy. We don't have to be in full agreement with the person. Our perception may differ from theirs, but that isn't what matters at that moment. What matters is being able to stay emotionally and relationally connected, even when it is hard for us. Here are a few examples of communicating with empathy:

1. A neurodivergent student yells "This is ridiculous – you never give me enough time to finish."
   a. Empathetic response: "It makes sense that you felt frustrated when I told you it was time to clean up. You were really excited to finish the project you were working on and you felt rushed. Thank you for letting me know what you were feeling. What is something we can do differently next time so you don't feel as rushed?"
   b. A non-empathetic response: "You are being dramatic and that isn't what happened. You need to tell the truth or I can't help you".
2. A colleague whose identities are societally marginalized, and are different from your identities, is venting to you about your principal—with whom you have a good relationship. They are expressing their frustration with feeling micromanaged and that it feels racially charged.
   a. Empathetic response: You set your own experience aside and say "Wow. Thank you for sharing that with me. That sounds so demoralizing. Is there anything I can do to support?".
   b. Nonempathetic response: "Well, I've never had that experience with our principal. Do you think you're just reading into it?".

Our capacity to tune into another person's emotional world, even when they are expressing something that generates discomfort for us, strengthens our relationships with other people and helps us grow.

Addressing Systemic Empathy Inequities

People are conditioned to experience empathy for people similar to them (Fowler et al. 2021). In schools with educators and administrators whose social identities do not match those of students, this needs to be acknowledged and addressed. Empathy is an emotional experience that we can expand and extend beyond people who have similar (or the same) social identities to us or those we care about, or for people with societal and positional power (e.g. himpathy).

We are more likely to experience empathy toward people similar to us in social identities and people who are close to us. This is one of the reasons we may struggle to believe that someone close to us could have said or done something harmful. We have a positive bias toward them and are more capable of seeing their full humanity.

Throughout history, people have categorized each other into "us vs. them." The mentality of "there are people like me who deserve protection and care, and there are people not like me who do not" is pervasive in our culture. As discussed in Chapter 8, our *positive social biases* can perpetuate unfair advantages. Empathy is an emotional resource that is not finite.

Pause & Reflect

Take a few minutes to reflect on selective empathy and compassion as it shows up within you and within your school and school system. This reflection can support you in identifying where systemic empathy is absent and needs tending. If it is helpful, take some time to use a mindfulness practice or any other practice to prepare your mind, body and heart to engage in this reflection.

1. First, reflect on the people in your school—youth and/or adults—with whom you feel a close relationship.
    a. What are their social identities?
        i. Are they the same or similar to yours?
    b. If they express upset or distress, what is your emotional response?
    c. What actions, if any, do you take?
2. Then take time to think about people in your school with whom you feel neutral.
    a. What are their social identities?
        i. Are they the same or similar to yours?

   b. If they express upset or distress, what is your emotional response?
   c. What actions, if any, do you take?
3. Then think about people in your school that you do not like (it's okay to not like everyone, including students. This just means you're a person; don't judge yourself).
   a. What are their social identities?
      i. Are they the same or similar to yours?
   b. If they express upset or distress, what is your emotional response?
   c. What actions, if any, do you take?

Take a few minutes to move around after completing this part of this reflection. Notice how you feel and the thoughts you might be having. Then take some time to reflect on organizational empathy.

1. Who in the school/school system is given "the benefit of the doubt?"
2. When people have conversations about "accountability," who in the school/school system is asked to be accountable for their actions?
3. Who in the school/school system is allowed to shirk responsibility and accountability?

If these answers aren't easy to answer, I invite you to look through any school-based data you have related to suspension, detention, and Hazing, Harassment, and Bullying (HHB) reports. Has any of the data changed over the years? If not, return to the questions above to consider why that data has not changed.

Affirmations to Challenge Emotional Bias

It can be helpful to use affirming statements when listening to someone's story in moments when we feel judgmental or dismissive of their experience. There is no universal truth and it is not our role to play detective, lawyer, or judge. The more capacity we have to provide soft and empathetic spaces for people to unburden their emotional tension, the softer our educational spaces will feel. Returning to the practice of embodied deep listening; listening with our whole selves with the intention to simply hear and understand, rather than react or solve, supports us in being more present and the person we are listening to feeling our presence.

Affirmations to Disrupt Biased Perceptions of Emotions

- It is important that I am curious about this person's emotional experience.
- Their emotions are not a problem; I can hold space for them.
- I might feel uncomfortable, but I can handle discomfort.
- My defensiveness might prevent me from understanding their message. I can soften.
- This person is complex like me.
- I don't need to know their whole story to know they deserve care.
- I might not understand their experience, but I can believe it.
- I might not be the person to offer care, but I know they are worthy of care.
- I do not need to like this person in order to see their humanity.
- My biases influence my beliefs about people. I can challenge and change my biases and beliefs.

CHAPTER SUMMARY

Just as we have been socialized to believe certain emotions are "good" and "bad," we have been socialized to believe and uphold notions of normalcy connected to emotional expression based on social identities. Identifying these biased perceptions of emotions, the impact they have, and working toward creating more room for emotional experiences and expression is part of building schools and school systems infused with justice and healing.

10

Addressing Control in Schools

Addressing Adultism in Education

Adultism is a particular kind of power imbalance we need to address in our educational spaces. As you read this next section, pay close attention to your emotional responses. Take note of the physical sensations and emotional experiences that surface.

Adultism is the belief that controlling children and youth is necessary and beneficial for them. In this form of *power over*, children and youth have little to no say in all or nearly all aspects of their lives (Tootoosis, 2020). John Bell (2018a) defines adultism as the "behaviors and attitudes based on the assumption that adults are better than young people and entitled to act upon young people without their agreement. This mistreatment is reinforced by social institutions, laws, customs, and attitudes" (p. 553).

Youth in schools are expected to comply with the rules set by adults. They are also far too often required to demonstrate respect for adults, even if the adults are showing disrespect toward them. This power imbalance means that youth are often required to be more accountable for themselves than the adults. Take some time to reflect on your upbringing. Use any mindfulness/grounding/centering practice that supports you in moving into a more relaxed and open state. Be aware of your thoughts, emotions, and physical sensations as you move through the questions.

DOI: 10.4324/9781003540687-11

Pause and Reflect

In your childhood, what were the expectations regarding respect toward adults? What if an adult was disrespectful to you? What happened? Who made the rules at home? Who made the rules at school? What happened if the rules were broken by youth? What happened if the rules were broken by adults? How did it feel if you did not get to be involved in making the rules? After reflecting, take some time to move your body and be with the thoughts and emotions that surfaced.

There is a constant dismissal of the experiences of children and youth, and adults may even proclaim "you're too young to understand." This dismissal denies children their full humanity, deserving of agency, autonomy, and being believed. Adultism coexists with other forms of oppression and is normalized throughout many cultures (Bell, 2018a; Tootoosis, 2020). Tootoosis (2020), a member of the Poundmaker Cree Nation, in his essay *The Cunning of the Adult Supremacist*, discussed the introduction of adult supremacy by colonization and the ongoing impact on Indigenous Nations and Indigenous youth. In his essay, he offers these questions as guides toward shifting from supremacy toward liberation:

> A simple approach is to relate to children like how you would relate to any other human being. What if children are equal? What if children are valuable regardless of where they are in their development? What if children can contribute to adult environments, ideas, and plans? What if children can creatively present solutions to problems?
>
> *(n.p.)*

Take a moment to pause, feel, and release an exhale. What are you feeling? What are you struggling with? What are you curious about? What is challenging you about this content? There is no right answer; there is just good information contained in your answers. If you are experiencing defensiveness, notice what that feels like, and take note of *what* you are defending. It may be helpful to revisit the shame shields as well as your beliefs and values.

Reflecting on Adultism

Adultism exists in schools. The level of our comfort or awareness with this truth varies. As you work to build a sense of how and where adultism may exist in your work with youth and in your school/workplace more broadly, take some time to respond to these questions:

1. How do you define "disrespect?"
2. How do you share power with students?
3. How do you demonstrate respect to students?
4. How do you expect students to show respect toward you?
5. When a student doesn't show you respect, based on your definition of respect, what emotions surface, and how does your nervous system respond?[1]
6. Which students do you find yourself engaging in power struggles with?
   a. Are their social identities the same or different from yours?
7. How do other educators in your school/workplace share power with students?
8. How do other educators demonstrate respect to students?
9. How do other educators expect students to show respect to them?
10. Which students do you see other educators engaging in power struggles with?
    a. What are the social identities of those educators and those students?
11. What is the impact on student–educator relationships when mutual respect is not present?
12. What would mutual respect between students and educators look like? Sound like? Feel like?
13. What is one way you would like to increase mutual respect between students and educators?

Who Needs to Be Accountable?

Building psychologically and emotionally justice-centered schools requires building adult emotional self-responsibility and accountability. Before we explore accountability, take a moment to reflect on your perceptions of accountability. When you think of "accountability," what is the first example that pops into your mind? What emotions surface for you when you think about accountability? What synonyms would you use for accountability? What does the phrase "they need to be held accountable" mean to you?

In my work with educators and adults, the practice of accountability is often punitive. I hear educators say "I want them to be accountable," and the hidden message is "I want them to be punished, reprimanded, scolded" in the forms of detention, suspension, or having the family informed. Accountability rarely, if ever, means "I want to help this student understand their actions and the impact they had on others. I want them to be held to a high standard because I know they are capable of doing better."

We learned about punishment and accountability through our familial, cultural, and school-based experiences. Take some time to reflect on these prompts and notice any emotional responses:

- In your upbringing, when you were held "accountable," what did that mean?
- Was it shame-based? Punitive? Was there ostracization?
- Who was asked to be accountable and who was not?

Were there any patterns that surfaced for you? Any "aha" moments? Take some time to move, breathe, or engage in a mindfulness practice after moving through this reflection.

Adultism = Adult Responsibility

Respect is sometimes a one-way street and there is a requirement that students are held *accountable* for their actions, words, and inactions, while educators and adults are exempt from the ways they are interacting with youth. A teacher can raise their voice at students, but a student cannot raise their voice toward adults without being punished. In an elementary school, students are required to walk silently through the halls, while adults are frequently having conversations with each other.

Take time to get centered with any practice before reading the below examples of interactions between adults and youth. As you read, take note of your thoughts, emotions, and physical sensations. Pause, if needed, to reconnect to the story.

A disabled and nonspeaking student who uses augmentative and alternative communication (AAC) on an iPad is sitting in the cafeteria. They start to experience sensory overload and begin to loudly vocalize. A staff member walks over to them, grabs their iPad and says "You need to calm down. I'll give this back when you're calm." The student becomes more distressed and tries to take their communication device back. The staff member says "You can't just grab things out of people's hands. You need to go to the office." The staff member writes up the student for "disrespectful behavior" and sends them to the office. The staff member tells the student's home room teacher about the interaction and the home room teacher sends an email home about the student's "disrespect toward adults."

A nonbinary and neurodivergent student has had trash thrown at and on them in the hallways between classes. This has happened multiple times. They have also been called dehumanizing names repeatedly. They do not want to report the students who are engaged in this behavior because they're afraid of more backlash. The students harassing them are on the basketball team and are beloved by the administrators. The guidance counselor who is supporting the nonbinary student is concerned because they are now doing worse with their classes and report not wanting to come to school. The principal says that "unless they give names, there's really nothing that can be done." The student says they will share that those kids are on the basketball team. The principal says "well, they're good boys, I'll talk to them." The next day, the principal is high-fiving the basketball players and congratulating them on their win. That same day the student has more trash thrown at them.

A Korean student is increasingly uncomfortable with a History teacher referring to Asian people as "Orientals." The teacher has also made "jokes" about Korean people eating dogs. The student gathers the courage to share this with an educator they trust in the school. The educator brings it to the principal, who says "Well, if the student has an issue, they really need to bring it up to that teacher." The educator asks the student if it would be okay to intervene on their behalf. The student agrees. The trusted educator talks with the history teacher, shares their own experiences of making missteps in the past and the discomfort they had when realizing the language they used was dehumanizing, and shares information about the term "Orientals" and food-based microaggressions. The history teacher nods a lot during their conversation. The next day in class, the History teacher spends most of class making passive aggressive comments, like "Well, I am not sure if I'm even allowed to say certain words anymore so I'm just going to avoid saying anything that might offend someone," and "I just wish my students knew that I care about all of them."

Pause & Reflect

- How did it feel reading these examples?
- What patterns did you notice?
- Are these scenarios familiar or unfamiliar to you?
- What are some other examples of ways in which you've seen adults be under-accountable and students be required to be over-accountable?
- In your school or school system, whose anger is taken seriously?
- Whose anger is deemed dangerous?
- Whose humanity is protected?
- Whose humanity is neglected?

After reflecting, take some time to move around. If you can, go outside, look out of a window, or use a mindfulness practice.

We need to be honest about our school expectations around emotional expression and the demand placed on youth in our schools. Far too often, we are creating a culture of control and suppression that hinders emotional growth and creates more distress.

Emotional Control of Youth

As a former speech language pathologist, I wrote unhelpful and, at times, harmful social and emotional skill development goals for students receiving services through an Individualized Education Program (IEP). These goals put a hyperfocus on a student being able to "regulate," "calm themselves," and "label their emotions" without addressing the environment that is creating or exacerbating "dysregulation." These goals do not support adults in recognizing how their own emotional state or dysregulation is contributing to the dysregulation of a student.

These goals also put an unequal amount of labor on neurodiverse students and other students experiencing bias and oppression, while their peers who have not been identified as neurodiverse and/or disabled do not have the same expectations. In fact, many students without disability labels struggle to express their current emotional states and also cannot "calm themselves" when they are frustrated. These students often receive more patience, compassion, curiosity, and collaborative problem-solving with adults, while neurodiverse and/or disabled students are more likely to be sent out of the classroom or even suspended for similar or identical behaviors their unidentified peers express (Diaz, 2015; Farinas, 2016; Shyman, 2016).

As a speech language pathologist, I used the Zones of Regulation © curriculum, which was created by an occupational therapist and autism resource specialist. I thoroughly enjoyed many parts of the curriculum. There was emphasis on promoting students in becoming more attuned to their physiological and emotional states and building a connection between the two. For example, if a student felt like their arms were heavy, that might help them realize they were tired. Or if they were tired, they were invited to think about how their body felt. That interoception development is so important in helping people of all ages become more aware of their inner world. However, the use of the Zones of Regulation can become a tool of control and compliance.

There are four different "zones" in this curriculum. According to the Zones of Regulation website (2023), the Blue Zone is when we have "low states of alertness and down feelings" and that "our energy is low and our body is moving slowly" (n.p.). The Green Zone "describes a calm, alert state. We may be feeling happy, focused, content, peaceful, or calm" (n.p.), while the

Yellow Zone is when "our emotions get a little stronger. We may be experiencing stress, frustration, anxiety, excitement, silliness, confusion, nervousness, be overwhelmed, or have the wiggles" (n.p.). They describe the Red Zone as

> a state of extremely high energy and intense, very overwhelming feelings. We may be in an extremely heightened state of alertness, potentially triggering our fight, flight, freeze or flee protective response. We may feel elated, euphoric, anger, rage, devastated, out of control, panicked, or terrified.
>
> *(n.p.)*

On this same page, they emphasize that "it's critically important that we don't convey the message that the Green Zone is the only acceptable Zone to be in. Acknowledge, accept, and support these feelings, never make anyone feel like the Green Zone is the norm" (n.p.). Yet, in many classrooms and in behavior plans, it is a common practice to reward students for being in the Green Zone. This happens when adults give tokens and/or compliments to students for being in the "Green Zone." It also happens when adults squash expressions of joy, excitement, silliness, and playfulness (yellow zone) by saying "Oh, it looks like you're in the yellow zone, let's take a deep breath so we can get back to the green zone." It is as if there is a fear of joy being expressed in our educational spaces.

Pause

Notice the emotions that are surfacing for you. Are you feeling guilt? Shame? Anger toward me? Disbelief? These emotions are useful and essential in understanding our habitual reactions. This discomfort, wherever it is coming from, holds important information. Perhaps you feel indignant at the ways you have seen youth treated but felt steamrolled by other people, and now you feel empowered to disrupt this even more. Conversely, you may feel disbelief that this is a problem, or you may feel angry at me. That defensiveness might indicate this is an area that you don't want to explore. Sitting with that discomfort and getting curious about *what* you are defending can provide some insight that is just behind that defensive wall.

Bias and Emotional Control Collide

In the previous chapter, we explored the ways we differently perceive emotions based on our biases. Our biases influence *who* we believe is "acting out" and who is "just being a kid." In order to create healthy and justice-centered spaces, we have to address these biases directly.

Example

Imagine this scenario. It is the end of a standardized assessment period. There are three students finishing a computer-based math assessment: a Black student, an East Asian student, and a White student. All three students are either receiving special education services or are in the process of being evaluated. All of them seem equally bored with the testing. All three students are stretching in their chairs, fidgeting, starting off into space, and, at various times, making groans and other vocalizations of boredom, frustration, and/or impatience. While they appear almost identical in their presentations of "I'm done with this boring testing," the responses from the educators in the classroom differ.

After one particularly loud sigh from the East Asian student, one of the three educators in the classroom calmly sits down next to the student. This educator says "You're doing such a great job. There's just a little more left. I know it's hard!" The educator then gets up and walks to the back of the room and stands with another teacher. The teacher then says loudly enough for the whole room to hear, "Isn't he doing such a great job?" and the other educator says, "Yes, he really is!"

The White student at one point seems to be melting out of their chair. Their chin is level with the edge of the desk and they are staring up at the ceiling. They let out a guttural "ahhhh!" A different teacher, not the one who tended to the East Asian student, walks over and encourages them to sit up in their chair. The teacher then gently rubs their back and asks them if they need a sensory tool. They get the student a weighted lap blanket and give some words of encouragement.

The Black student has nearly identical presentations of expressions of boredom and doneness with this assessment. At one point they exclaim "I can't do this!" no louder than either of the other two students who had used groans to communicate, rather than words. A third educator in the room swiftly walks over to this student, stands over them and says with a harsh delivery, "If you need help you need to say *I need help*." The waves of frustration coming from the teacher are palpable. The Black student is not offered encouragement; nor are they offered any sensory tools. They are instead reprimanded for doing exactly what their same-aged peers were doing. The only difference is they are Black. Which student do you think gets sent to the principal's office for "disrespect and defiance"?

This example highlights multiple factors; racial bias and adult responses that contribute to the devaluation of a student. As adults, we need to be responsible for our interactions with students and be unflinching in our ability to identity-based biased responses to students. It is untenable that students are required to be respectful to adults who are treating them disrespectfully.

Make Room for Emotions

Far too often in schools, both youth and adults are chastised for any emotional expression outside of happy, focused, attentive, and grateful. These emotional expectations ingrained in many schools are organized around sameness and compliance. In observations and conversations with teachers, many schools employ strategies to control student emotions. Frequently, when a student expresses anger, frustration, annoyance, or any other emotion frequently labeled as "negative," they are told they need to stop feeling that feeling. This response, in turn, heightens that emotion.

One of my least favorite phrases I hear is "You get what you get and you don't get upset." I understand the idea; we want students to move on from feeling upset that they didn't get the purple folder. However, a student can be upset and we can teach them ways to name the upset. We could also allow for a 1–2-minute swap if needed so that students get the color they want. Our interpretation of students' emotions as manipulative (e.g. statements of beliefs like "they're just trying to get their way" or "they're just trying to be difficult") is detrimental to our relationships with them. We cannot expect youth to be able to self-regulate in ways adults aren't even always able to do. Working in schools is emotionally laborious – as we discussed earlier and as you well know. The level of emotional labor and multitasking that takes place in a school day is unconscionable. When we can intentionally center ourselves, it reduces our stress responses and can influence the energy of the room. This is the power of co-regulation.

Co-Regulation

Have you had the experience when someone is fully listening to you and they feel your feelings with you (aka *empathy*)? What does that feel like? How does your body feel? This is co-regulation in action. A nervous system that is in a state of *rest and digest* can support someone else's nervous system in a state of *fight/flight* or *freeze* to move toward a state of *rest and digest*. If we are able to slow ourselves down in the moment and use mini-practices, we are more likely to be able to be responsive rather than reactive.

Take a moment to recall a moment in your day when you *reacted* rather than *empathetically responded* to someone's emotional state. Reactions could include: trying to solve it; trying to put a positive spin on their story; giving them advice; telling them to relax. Empathetic responses might include: "That sounds tough, is there something I can do?," "That's a strong feeling; it makes sense you're feeling that way," "Wow, thank you for telling me, I'm going to take a deep breath after feeling how hard that was for you". What happened for the person when you *reacted*?

Sometimes it feels as if we can just get someone to "snap out" of their emotion, we can move on with our day, our lesson plan, etc. However, it rarely results in us feeling balanced or the people around us feeling balanced. There will be many times you cannot hold space for someone's emotions, and that is okay. However, if we can make shifts toward *empathetic responses* and away from *reactions* we may actually discover what support will be helpful and move out of unnecessary power struggles. Our nervous systems will also be grateful for not being pushed into a heightened or agitated state.

"Just Calm Down"

Have you ever been sharing your anger or frustration or disappointment about something with someone and they say something like "It's not that big of a deal" or "Maybe you should just take a deep breath." What happens to your emotional state when you receive messages like that? It isn't helpful to try to squash someone's emotional world.

This is the opposite of attunement and co-regulation. It is detachment and rejection. It is much like the ignore procedure – ignoring unwanted behaviors – is one often used especially for students who have intense emotional displays. Emotional detachment is an approach that can heighten an emotional response rather than release it. This happens regularly for students in our care.

The Cost of Controlling Student Emotions

Students who have been identified by adults as needing a behavior plan are most frequently the students who are secluded. There was a student I used to work with who had one of these behavior plans. If she displayed any emotions that were even slightly elevated, she was warned to get into a calmer state or she would go to the seclusion room.

This student was a younger elementary-age student with an assigned 1:1; an adult who was almost glued to her throughout her entire day. The 1:1 carried a clipboard and took data on her all day. At one point the student realized that she was being watched. She looked at the 1:1 and said "Stop writing notes about me." The adults labeled her as "paranoid" and the educators supervising the 1:1 instructed them to tell the student they were not writing about her. The 1:1 was instructed to lie to a child. The student became increasingly frustrated because the 1:1 kept insisting they were not writing notes about her while they were writing notes and then was sent to the seclusion room.

One of my roles was to be part of the crisis team and I was called to support the student. I went to the seclusion room and sat in the room while the student paced across the small windowless room that was formerly a supply closet. She was understandably agitated and kept saying "They are lying to me. Why are they lying to me?" I nodded my head and offered her validation and said "That is really frustrating." She looked surprised that I said anything to her and then after a little while, she sat down near me. I didn't have a chance to talk more with her because I was then tagged out by someone on her educational team.

After I was tagged out, the person in charge of writing her behavior plan took me aside and let me know that I didn't follow the proper protocol. They informed me that the behavior plan stated that when the student was agitated, adults were supposed to ignore her until she calmed down. I was essentially reprimanded for not emotionally harming a child and for providing empathy, compassion, and honesty.

This story is not unlike many stories that educators have of the rigid control they are expected to exert over students. The above story is a perfect example of that. In addition to needing to not be gaslit by the adults, the student also needed to have her emotional experience validated and not negated. By negating her very real distress through a behavior plan, it heightened her distress and led to adults feeling justified in using a physical intervention and putting this child in a windowless room alone and in distress. This is trauma-inducing and disabled students and students of the Global Majority are the ones who are most at risk of being subjected to this type of trauma-inducing experience (ACLU, 2019). We can—and must—do better.

Practice: Moving from Reaction to Response

Visualization practices can support us in building mental and physiological maps on ways we would like to show up in future situations. These practices are not about planning exactly what you will say, what the other people will say, and somehow magically the day, the meeting, the lesson go perfectly. Rather, this is a way to build in different habits so we can respond rather than react.

Find a distraction-reduced space. Take a few moments to settle in with your own practice or one of the foundational or mini-practices from Chapter 1. Recall a moment that you *reacted* to a student or a colleague or a student's family member rather than *responded* to their emotional expression. Notice what your body feels like. Notice the emotions. Take a few breaths. Then shift and think about how you would like to respond to a similar situation in the future. Visualize yourself offering an *empathetic response* in the same or similar situation. Notice what your body feels like. Notice the emotions. Take a few breaths.

What did you notice? What differences did you experience? What worries do you have about giving an *empathetic response* vs. a *reaction*? Then bring this into your day(s). Experiment with different *empathetic responses* that feel authentic to you and take note of how the situation unfolds afterwards.

Pause and Reflect

If it is helpful and there is time, use one of the foundational or mini-mindfulness practices before reflection. Then respond to these prompts:

- Are the tools we use to understand students and their behaviors rooted in compassion or compliance?
- Are the ways we interact with students demonstrating mutual respect or demanding that students respect authority?
- How does adultism impact the emotional expression and humanity of Black students, disabled students, and other societally marginalized students?
- What do we need to do differently?

Take some time to process your reflection in a way that feels supportive through movement or rest. Then notice how your body feels and the emotions that are surfacing as you read through your reflection.

Affirmations to Disrupt Control in Schools

- ♦ Youth hold inherent wisdom.
- ♦ Power struggles create a no-win for everyone.
- ♦ Learning from the insights youth have can transform our schools and our world.
- ♦ I don't have to replicate how I was raised.
- ♦ I trust the stories of young people.
- ♦ I believe young people and work to make changes alongside them.

- I co-create spaces where young people can share their perspectives without fear.
- I can be a trustworthy adult for young people.

Note

1 There are some situations in which young educators and student educators are in a very complicated dynamic when teaching high school students. For example, a group of nonbinary and women student teachers shared that they would often experience belligerent behavior from some of the young men in their classrooms. They described feeling alone and uncertain of how to address this behavior. This gendered power imbalance is something that needs close attention so that these young teachers are not experiencing harm. Educating young men to not enact domination over others they have been socialized to view and treat as "lesser than" is the key to disrupting this. Be aware that this is also especially pertinent to young educators whose experiences with ableism, racism, xenophobia, and other forms of oppression are also present.

CHAPTER SUMMARY

Adultism is a form of *power over* that puts pressure on youth to conform and comply with adult rules and expectations even when those rules and expectations are harmful or hurtful. Bias and biased perceptions of emotions influences the control exerted over youth of the Global Majority and disabled youth. We can learn to soften and provide *empathetic responses* rather than *reactive responses* to create more ease for ourselves and the people we are responding to. This can reduce power struggles and create educational spaces where students are respected.

11

Creating a Culture to Engage in Collaborative Changework

Creating a Culture to Engage in Changework

We truly need each other to facilitate change at the personal, interpersonal, and systemic levels and we very much need our wellness and wholeness in order to create change rooted in healing and justice. Reflection and humility are required when confronting and addressing workplace environments, policies and practices and leadership styles that are trauma-inducing as discussed in the previous chapters. In order to support sustained change, we need collaborative relationships and a culture that supports our work of engaging in important, and, at times, uncomfortable conversations.

Building Systems for Supportive Feedback

There is a wide variety of formal and informal feedback within school systems for educators. Some feedback systems are reliant on a principal or other administrator pre-scheduling two observation times throughout the school year. For each observation, the educator provides a comprehensive lesson plan before the observation and then a rubric is completed by both the administrator and the educator. The two then meet and discuss the evaluation results. There are many issues with this model.

DOI: 10.4324/9781003540687-12

Two observations in a school year does not capture the full range of the responsibilities of educators. This misses: family–teacher conferences, team meetings, among other aspects of the many roles and responsibilities educators perform throughout the year. With a model like this, educators are formally observed for one to two hours out of a 1,350-hour school year (calculated for full-time, 180-day school year at 7.5 hours/day). This means educators are observed and evaluated on 0.75% to 1.4% of the work they do in a highly structured and pre-planned way. Since this evaluation model results in observations that occur every three years, this reduces those percentages to 0.25% and 0.46%, respectively. This is hardly enough time to identify strengths and challenges and to support the refinement and growth of professional skills.

A formal evaluation every three years does not promote or support a culture organized around learning and growth; it becomes a process of going through the motions. Rather than differentiating and ensuring the right types of support needed for each educator, this approach is based on a fixed "ideal" educator and holds everyone to the same standard.

Take a moment to think about the ways you do or do not receive supportive feedback in your role. Who provides feedback? How often? Is it feedback or critique? Does it help you grow as a professional? Does it feel growth-oriented or punitive?

Giving and Receiving Feedback with Grace

We can learn so much from each other, and we have so much to offer other people. Learning how to give and receive feedback with grace is an incredibly powerful opportunity to be challenged and to change habits and practices that are not working for us or for those we are working with, youth or adults.

In my role as a consultant, I have the honor of watching lessons in real time. I get to witness the amazing pedagogical moves and relationship development happening in classrooms. I also have the opportunity to see places where shifts could be beneficial for everyone in the space. Not everyone has access to a consultant or a coach. There are some schools that prioritize peer observations and collaboration; others do not because there is no time. Educators are some of the most creative people and they would be able to rework a schedule to create opportunities for peer observation and collaboration. In the meantime, videos can be a powerful way to reflect on your work with others.

I encourage educators to set up their phone (with the correct permissions according to your school/school system policies) and record themselves teaching or facilitating a meeting for 5–10 minutes. The recordings should capture different parts of the day and/or different groups of students. The recordings should be zoomed out enough so a wide view of the educational space can be seen.

It is a vulnerable and courageous endeavor to ask people "What do you see that I don't?" and "Do you have ideas about what I could do differently?" Embedding this practice into your team meetings and/or creating collaborative opportunities to engage in this reflection practice is incredibly impactful.

The Purpose of Feedback

The purpose of feedback is to support growth and change. It is not to shame, blame, or try to influence someone to teach, lead, or facilitate the way you do. It is an opportunity for building self-awareness and situational awareness. Other people can see what we cannot and have ideas that can be beneficial for us. The previous chapter can support us in building more capacity to be with the discomfort that inevitably arises when we receive feedback.

We Need Each Other to Understand Ourselves

One of my favorite stories I tell people is about the time my partner and I were in an argument in the car. I was convinced that I was calm, cool, and collected. I was convinced he was being combative. Then I happened to see my reflection in the side-view mirror and how I *thought* I was acting and how I was *actually* acting were entirely different. My brow was furrowed and my mouth was narrowed. I looked furious because I was. But I was able to convince myself into believing that I was being patient and rational while *he* was being combative. The truth was, we both were, but I was unaware of the state of my own nervous system. It was such a powerful reminder that we truly need mirrors—sometimes actual mirrors and sometimes other people being honest with us—to know how we are actually showing up in the world.

Receiving Feedback

It is important that you understand your own feedback style preferences so that you can communicate to others how you best receive feedback. Some people want very direct feedback like "You should try xyx next time." Other people prefer being asked open-ended questions so they can guide their own learning. It is often beneficial to be accepting of a combination of both.

For some people, it might be helpful to watch the recordings first on your own and take note of what you noticed; what you thought worked, what could use some refining, and what you're curious about. The questions embedded in Chapters 8, 9 and 10 can be helpful tools to reflect on how bias, biased perceptions, and adultism are present in any space. We can and must build the capacity to bring our nervous systems into a state of *rest and digest* when engaging in these conversations and reflections. Building and co-creating community agreements can support a team or group of people in building the capacity to do this beautifully challenging work together. We can also reflect on these questions:

- Whose teaching approaches/pedagogies do I admire?
- How could I try some of those approaches in my work?
- What support would be helpful?

In addition to getting supportive feedback, we need spaces that are organized around supporting people in learning how to share space in ways that support growth, make room for difference, and ensure that conversations around justice and healing are not sidelined. One way to do this is by developing community agreements or ethos.

Co-Creating Community Agreements/Ethos

Community agreements or ethos are used with varying levels of success across educational settings, whether it is a high school classroom or a staff meeting. There are many ways in which these are used to stifle dissent and to uphold notions of "politeness." For example, an educator shared a story of being in a staff meeting that got contentious. At the next meeting, the principal gave everyone a list of "25 rules" for meetings. There was no discussion about any of the rules, nor was there buy-in. As discussed in Chapter 7, this is a form of *power-over* leadership and prevents necessary generative conflict. This tactic will exacerbate feelings of overwhelm, powerlessness, and frustration amongst those who are being asked to comply with rules. We need collaboratively-developed agreements and agreements suited for different situations and purposes.

Some people use the same agreements or norms in all settings for all meetings, which also doesn't often work. We need responsive and adaptable community agreements and ethos depending on the group and the reason the group is together. Community agreements for a meeting with families should be different than ones used with a long-standing team.

In my work, rather than "agreements" or "norms," I use "ethos," which the Oxford Dictionary (2025) defines as "the characteristic spirit of a culture, era, or community as manifested in its beliefs and aspirations" (n.p.). Co-created ethos provide guidance and reminders to us about how we want to be in community with each other. Essential elements of ethos are:

- They address power dynamics in a space.
- They are developed as a group process.
- They are revisited regularly with reflection that includes:
  - How are we currently practicing these?
  - Which ones do we need to recommit to?
  - What needs to be changed or added?
- Create psychological and emotional safety.

Psychological safety is a term coined by Dr. Amy Edmondson. In her 1999 paper, she wrote that psychological safety is present when "people are comfortable expressing and being themselves" and that it is "safe for interpersonal risk taking—that one will not be embarrassed, rejected, or punished for speaking up with ideas, questions, concerns, or mistakes" (p. 354). Similarly, *emotional safety* is present when someone experiences the ability to express their emotions and be vulnerable without fear of social rejection or punishment. It is always important to remember that different expectations around emotional expression are connected to social identities (Chapters 8 and 9) and to remember the different origins of anger. Emotional safety does not mean that people can respond ragefully when being asked to address an injustice. It means that people can talk about injustices with anger and frustration without fear of rage being directed their way. It is essential to remember that *safety* does not mean the absence of tension or discomfort. There will be more on this in Chapters 12 and 13.

Expectations vs. Ethos

Ethos should feel like they are simultaneously generating hope and providing guidance on how to navigate conflict when it arises. Ethos are not rules. They are invitations and reminders to individuals and a group about how we are sharing space. There are some expectations that are rules rather than ethos. For example, people often want to include statements like "we are on time for meetings" or "we show up to meetings prepared" in ethos. These are rules and can feel compliance-based (e.g. follow these rules or you will experience some passive-aggressiveness or be told you're not adhering to our *ethos*).

If someone is chronically late, the first step to addressing that is to speak with the person to get more information. Lateness may originate from a variety of reasons, but if the impulse is to believe it is because they are noncompliant and/or doing it on purpose, we are making assumptions which rarely leads to resolution or understanding. Lateness can stem from having the meeting at a time that is inconvenient because of other responsibilities, neurodivergence, and/or different cultural relationships to time.

Conversations about time and relationships to time can help the group understand what adjustments and modifications can be made to be responsive to the needs of the individuals within the group. If lateness is connected to a person not valuing the meeting because it feels like a waste of their time, conversations can be had to address this openly. Passive-aggressive maneuvers, like intentionally showing up late, are sometimes used as an attempt to gain control over situations in which it feels like there is no control. Again, open conversations to surface what is at the root of lateness will result in a better understanding of what needs to be done to adjust.

Another common "rule" disguised as an element of a groups' ethos is "we show up to meetings prepared." Similar to the time rule, there are myriad reasons why someone may seem "unprepared" for a meeting. Engaging in open dialogue about the different roles people have within the school can be helpful in gaining perspective. Not everyone has the time and space to review long meeting notes because of their various professional roles and personal lives. We also do not need to know the details of someone's personal life to be generously accommodating. Our stories are not owed to anyone. Adjusting and addressing the root causes of perceived "unpreparedness" can lead to adapting the expectations so that people are able to participate to the best of their capacity.

If you are short on time, I suggest offering samples to the group at the beginning of the meeting. Then ask people if there are questions or comments. After that, invite people to share other agreements that would be helpful for them. This last part is especially important when meeting with families and/or caregivers. Their meaningful input is necessary and the meetings with them are rarely long enough to co-develop agreements.

Avoid Weaponizing Agreements

When tensions rise in a meeting or in a classroom, it can be very tempting to point to the agreements and say something like "Remember, we agreed to treat each other with respect" or "You're not paying attention and that is not how we show up for each other." These messages may land as controlling and condescending.

Agreements such as "We assume good intentions" can often inadvertently evade necessary conversations around justice issues in schools. The belief that talking about the presence of racism, sexism, xenophobia in policies, practices, and personal interactions is "assuming bad intentions" can create an environment that evades and avoids these conversations.

Community agreements/ethos that support a group in directly addressing injustice issues encourage people to learn about defensive maneuvers and to be responsible for their own defensiveness.

Building Justice-Centered Community Agreements/Ethos

As we have explored throughout this book, power differentials surface in a variety of ways in schools. Recently, a teacher shared they didn't see any power differentials in the group I was facilitating. It was a group of classroom teachers, academic support specialists, and behavior support specialists. There were age differences, and there was one multiracial person and the rest of the staff were White. Those were the observable differences in power.

In addition to those social group memberships, power differentials are present when there is a difference in seniority, position within the union (e.g. a president/leader of a union compared to a union member), administrator, number of advanced degrees, and so on. These power imbalances do not always lead to people with less power in a situation to be hesitant to speak up, but they can impede full presence and authenticity.

Addressing Tone Policing and Evasion

In Chapter 9, we uncovered some of the ways emotional expression is gendered and racialized. Tone policing will also show up in weaponized agreements. Tone policing is exactly what the name implies; it is attempting to control *how* someone is expressing themselves. Tone policing is a control and evasion tactic designed to evade and avoid the topic at hand that may be uncomfortable for someone.

The underlying message of tone policing is "If you said it nicer, maybe I would listen." If someone is angry about experiencing or witnessing any form of harm and/or oppression, they do not need to "nicen" the tone. The reality is, even if people share their anger about racism, sexism with people, especially people with dominant social identities, it is the content that creates discomfort. There is no tone change that will change the quality of someone's listening. The left side of the chart below shows examples of direct communication and the middle column shows examples of tone policing. The column on the right provides examples of other evasion tactics. After you read through the chart, pause and take note of how you feel, especially feelings of discomfort or agitation.

Direct Communication	*Tone Policing Response*	*Other Evasion Tactics*
"Mistaking me for the only other Black person in the school is a microaggression."	"Can we not call it a *microaggression?* That just seems so harsh."	"I just think you need to stop looking for things to be upset about. This is ridiculous."
"I am very upset that we keep seeing our Black students sent to the Principal's office and we haven't done anything to change this."	"Look, if you would stop raising your voice maybe I would listen to you."	"Well, we are looking at the data, aren't we? That's doing something. It's not like we aren't doing anything. Let's be positive here."
"I'm concerned that nearly one-third of students in this grade are being referred for special education evaluations. A group of us have talked about how the new math program seems too fast and the behavior referrals spike during math."	"I don't think you should be so negative about that new math program. There is a lot of really good research about it."	"I don't know why you are blaming the program. It's the kids. They just can't sit still. They need to learn how to control themselves."

Co-Creating Ethos

If you are working on a team or within a group, I suggest starting by co-creating agreements/ethos before starting this work. I often used the word *ethos*, which Merriam-Webster defines as "the distinguishing character, sentiment, moral nature, or guiding beliefs of a person, group, or institution" (2025), rather than community agreements. However, you should choose the language that works best for your setting.

The following reflection practice should be done individually first. These reflection questions will be supportive in building and co-creating community agreements/ethos for engaging in conversations about identity and power. Be transparent that these responses will not be kept private. After people have an opportunity to reflect for themselves, allow people to share in small groups.

1. I learn best when…
2. I feel supported by others in my learning when…
3. When I feel uncomfortable, do I often avoid (flee)? get defensive (fight)? shut down (freeze)?…
4. Growing up, this is how conversations about racism, ableism, sexism, and other forms of oppression went…
5. I describe my comfort level with conversations about racism, ableism, sexism, and other forms of oppression as…
6. What would a supportive space feel like?
   a. How can I contribute to the space being supportive?
   b. How can others contribute to the space feeling supportive?
7. How could we navigate the discomfort with my and our complicity with racism, ableism, sexism, and other forms of oppression?
8. How do I think we can tackle conversations about race, racism, disability, ableism, sexism, and other forms of oppression and prejudice that are omnipresent in society and therefore our schools?

There may be someone (or a couple of people) within the team who are particularly skilled at synthesizing information. Lovingly charge them with the task of building a short list of tangible, actionable, and observable community agreements. After they share the completed list with the group, the group will provide feedback and input on any language changes that might be helpful. These agreements should not be viewed as permanent. They should be revisited and revised as the conversations deepen. They should also be revisited and revised when new people join a team or group.

If you are very short on time (as most people working in education are), you can use predeveloped community agreements/ethos and use them as a starting point to then revise and update to meet the needs of your particular group. Sample agreements are below:

Sample Community Agreements/Ethos:

1. Each of us is a unique constellation of identities. Who we are is important and influences how we perceive the world and how the world perceives us. We honor each other by honoring the ways people name themselves.
2. We are willing to engage to the best of our capacity which is different each day. We reduce distractions (phones, laptops put away). Be as vulnerable as is comfortable and know that your presence or lack of presence impacts the group.
3. We make space for intent and take ownership for impact by honoring what the person impacted needs. We uncover and address power imbalances.
4. We listen to others with our whole self with openness, curiosity and compassion rather than to debate or critique. We are aware of how you listen (seek to understand rather than debate).
5. We invite your emotions to be present and take responsibility for our defensiveness.
6. We acknowledge our own and each other's imperfections and offer ourselves and each other grace and humility. It isn't about getting it "right" but about learning from our mistakes. We create room for the discomfort of making mistakes and repairing.
7. We recognize our own biases and judgments as they come up. We are curious and compassionate with ourselves and reflect on why they exist and how they are influencing our perceptions.
8. Confidentiality – we do not share stories that are not our own, especially of those by historically marginalized people. The storyteller holds the power of when, what and how to share information.

Revisit and Revise

Community agreements/ethos should not be treated as rigid guidelines or signed documents that give the sense that they are legally binding. It is important to revisit them and revise them as you continue to move through work with a group or on a team. As you work with the community agreements/ethos, take note of what seems to be working well: *are people embracing these? How do we know?* It is also important to identify changes that could be made: *people seem to be interpreting this agreement differently, could we change the wording?* There are times when some agreements need to be completely scrapped or new ones need to be added. After-meeting check-ins on what worked well and what needs adjusting for future meetings can be one place these conversations begin. It is also helpful to schedule a longer amount of time every two or three months to revisit and move through a revision process as a team if necessary.

Multiracial Space Considerations

In Derald Wing Sue's (2016) book, *Race Talk and the Conspiracy of Silence: Understanding and Facilitating Difficult Dialogues on Race*, he unpacks the complex nature of engaging in conversations about race. He notes the multilayered reasons people of color struggle to engage in conversations about race in multiracial spaces with White people. These reasons include:

> a) determining how to talk about the elephant in the room when Whites avoid acknowledging it; b) dealing with the denial, defensiveness, and anxiety emanating from their White counterparts; c) managing their intense anger at the continued denial; and d) needing to constantly ascertain how much to open up, given the differential power dynamics that often exist.
>
> *(p. 34)*

Sue also details the origins of avoidance in talking about race and racism for White people as being connected to the following: "a) silence allows the maintenance of a false belief in one's own racial innocence; b) avoidance of personal blame for the oppression of others; and c) allows White people to dodge their responsibility in disrupting racism and oppression" (p. 34). Consider the origins of any discomfort that arises for you connected to your own social identities as you read on. It can be helpful to revisit Chapter 3 and to reflect on your emotional and nervous system responses.

At times, people with dominant social identities will describe their proximity to societally marginalized identities based on their relationships. A White woman will talk about her Black adopted son, or a non-disabled person will describe their relationship to their disabled sibling. While these experiences can provide insight into the experiences of being Black and adopted or of being disabled because of the closeness of the relationship, that does not mean that these people can claim to "get it" or "know what it's like" because of their proximity. Similarly, a White educator working in a predominantly Black, Latine, multilingual, and multicultural setting does not mean they are an expert in the experiences of students and families with whom they are in relationship. The only people who are experts of their experiences are the people experiencing it themselves. It is also necessary to understand the way whiteness operates in our culture.

The following definition of whiteness and white racial identity is from a post no longer available from the National Museum of African American History and Culture:

> Whiteness and white racialized identity refer to the way that white people, their customs, culture, and beliefs operate as the standard by which all other groups are compared. Whiteness is also at the core of understanding race in America. Whiteness and the normalization of white racial identity throughout America's history have created a culture where non-white persons are seen as inferior or abnormal. This white-dominant culture also operates as a social mechanism that grants advantages to white people, since they can navigate society both by feeling normal and being viewed as normal. Persons who identify as white rarely have to think about their racial identity because they live within a culture where whiteness has been normalized.

Take a moment to pause and reflect on what this means for you and your socialization. Notice any emotional responses. For White readers in particular, take note of any sticky emotions surfacing. It is essential to continuously grapple with your own emotional responses as you unlearn and find new ways of moving through the world.

Building Authentic Relationships

Engaging in meaningful relationships with people with experiences different from your own and learning from them requires a beautiful mix of humility, reflection, deep listening, curiosity, and a willingness to have your worldview challenged and ultimately changed. When I am in company with people whose experiences are different from my own (e.g., trans, Black, disabled, first generation immigrants), I work to soften my shoulders and my stomach and to then relax my whole body. From that soft and receptive space, I invite their stories to wash over me. I catch myself when I am trying to predict the direction of their stories; I return to their words, their voice, and their experiences. I stay centered and present in my own body while tending to their story with receptivity and open curiosity. I may find there are simultaneous similarities and oceans of difference between our experiences. In order to fully communicate that I understand their world and experiences, I focus more on what they said rather than how it relates to me. That doesn't mean I never find ways to say "I connected with this piece of your experience," but it does mean that I don't take those similarities as opportunities to say "we're the same," or as an invitation to talk about myself.

If you hear someone share their named identity that you are unfamiliar with, it is your work to believe and validate that person's identity; not to explain why their self-naming is wrong. For example, there are people who self-identify as fat. We live in a fatphobic society that sends messages that fat people are unhealthy, despite vast research that has disproved this time and time again (Nagoski & Amelia Nagoski, 2020), and in turn, tries to dissuade people from claiming their own self-descriptors such as fat. As another example, I identify as biracial and racially/ethnically ambiguous. There are mixed-race people who vehemently push back against this phrase, as is their right. I have no interest nor intention in trying to convince anyone with whom

I share that particular identity that they should choose my way of naming myself. I also have to educate myself on why people push back against that phrase.

For many years in education, there was a push to be "person-centered" and to use language like "person with a disability." However, many people within that community preferred "disabled." I highly recommend reading the work of disability activists rather than non-disabled academics when seeking to be respectful of people's identities. Similarly, read the works and ideas from people within a group rather than from people outside the group when it comes to learning the language that is respectful. There are social identity words and phrases that have been reclaimed by people within those particular groups and would still be considered hurtful and a slur if used by people who are not within the group. Ta-Nehisi Coates (2017) has a great video that explains why he will not use a specific word when greeting his wife's friends, and that he has no right to tell them to *not* use that word. The rest of the video is about the use of a word no one outside of the Black community has a right to use. I highly encourage you to watch and/or listen to this.

In schools and educational organizations that are predominantly White, developing affinity spaces for this work is essential. These affinity spaces can either be in addition to the multiracial work being done across a school or educational organization or in replacement of that work. It should be determined by the educators of the Global Majority as to how they would like to participate. People may have different comfort levels so not everyone may be engaging in the work the same way and we need to create avenues for choice.

Pause and Reflect

Take a few minutes to reflect on this chapter. Perhaps you work in a setting that already has many of these practices in place. How might this chapter help shift or refine some of the practices in your setting? If your school/school system is lacking in collaborative change systems, take some time to notice your response to this chapter. Do you feel overwhelmed? Hopeful? Cynical? Be curious toward any emotional responses that are surfacing.

Practice TONAL: *Tune in, Observe sensations & thoughts, Name the emotion and experience, Allow the emotion to move, Loving response to self* as you move through your emotions.

Affirmations for Collaboration

- Collective wisdom is more important than individual gain.
- I have something to learn from everyone.
- While feedback may be uncomfortable, it can help me to understand myself more fully.
- I know myself better than anyone else and I can listen to people's perceptions without crumbling.
- I don't have to agree with everyone.
- Multiple perspectives can co-exist.
- I can stay steady and focused on disrupting harm and any feedback designed to diminish me rather than support my growth.
- I am discerning with the information I take in and whose opinions I trust.
- Building authentic relationships with people requires that I believe them when they tell me who they are.

CHAPTER SUMMARY

Changework cannot be reliant on one person enacting change. We need supportive and collaborative relationships in our schools and school systems. We can create opportunities to give and receive meaningful feedback to identify where bias is present in our work and to change our practices. We also need to co-create spaces where we can engage in meaningful conversations about issues within the system and understand each other more fully.

12

Engaging in Generative Conflict

Conflict Engagement

Conflict is a normal phenomenon that happens in all relationships. The ways we engage in conflict can be supportive to growth and change or they can lead to an increase in mistrust and a lack of psychological safety. Our individual conflict patterns are connected to our upbringings and our socialization. Your individual conflict patterns and preferences may be very different from those of your broader workplace cultural conflict patterns.

When you think of conflict, what is the first thing that pops into your mind? How does your body feel? What emotions are you experiencing? This chapter is designed to build an understanding of your own relationship to conflict, the rules of conflict within your school/school system, and to dream up ways that generative conflict could exist more in your school/school setting.

One Big Happy Family

I often hear educators talk about their team or their whole building as "one big family." The belief behind this is that "everyone gets along" and "we all like each other." I countered that if any non-familial group really was "one big family," then they had a lot of family therapy to go to. As we keep exploring throughout

DOI: 10.4324/9781003540687-13

this book, we bring our histories with us to education. Our history in relation to our emotions, our history of socialization, and the relationships we had during our formative years and the ones we have now. Similarly, we bring the type of conflict styles we were explicitly and implicitly taught.

A team I consulted with who did label themselves as being "like a family" did indeed show family-like qualities. During the meeting when we were all present, everyone talked over each other, interrupted each other, and one person had to leave midway through the meeting to tend to another task. When that person left, the other two people almost immediately started talking about how frustrated they were with the now-absent person for always being late to meetings. I asked them if they ever talked about it directly, and they said "Oh, no I guess we haven't."

School/School System Culture

Many years ago, when I facilitated a workshop, I mentioned that it is important to reflect on how well or unwell people are within a school/school system and that it can be helpful to consider the culture. One of the participants, who worked in a fairly large school, said "Well, we all get along, and we all love our jobs, so my school is a great place to work." In my statement, I didn't indicate that anyone's school or school system was a "bad place to work" or that "people were just constantly fighting." Nor did I say that "everyone hates their jobs." This is one of many reasons why understanding and reflecting on the many ways our defensiveness shows up is helpful as we continue to gain a more nuanced understanding of the education system we work within. It may be helpful to reflect on these questions over the course of a few days or even weeks. Sometimes it is challenging to really get a sense of the culture that we have come to feel is "normal".

- Do people directly engage in conflict and disagreements?
- Or do people talk behind each other's backs instead of direct conversations?
- Is there "one way" people are expected to engage in conflict?

- Are there hidden or explicit expectations that people "go along to get along" even when the issue has not been addressed?
- When there are disagreements or conflict, are people labeled as "difficult" or "unprofessional"?
- If someone names a practice, curriculum, lesson plan as racist, ableist, etc. do people engage in meaningful discussion? Or are people told to "stop being negative" or "stop making everyone about identity"?

Once you have compiled your thoughts, whether it was in one reflection or across a few weeks, take some time to describe your school/workplace climate and culture. It can be challenging to get a clear understanding of the hidden culture within a school or workplace. Everything just feels "normal." While it may feel familiar, that doesn't mean it is healthy. If you are working on a team, it may be helpful to use this practice together.

We gain important insight when we learn from other perspectives. Revisit the social identity work, and see if there are patterns of differential treatment based on social identities. An honest assessment of the climate and culture we are influenced by and influencing helps us find the paths out of unhealthy or dysfunctional patterns and practices.

Our Personal Relationship to Conflict

Let's take a little quiz. This isn't a quiz where you get points, and then you find out your conflict style. Those do exist, and this isn't that. The purpose is to be in honest, and potentially uncomfortable, reflection about how you currently do/do not engage in conflict.

In this quiz, go with your gut response. Don't overthink it!

Conflict Quiz: Your Relationship with Conflict	*1 = not true at all; 5 = very true*				
I am comfortable mediating conflict between other people.	1	2	3	4	5
I am comfortable with interpersonal conflict when I have made a mistake.	1	2	3	4	5

Conflict Quiz: Your Relationship with Conflict	*1 = not true at all; 5 = very true*				
I am comfortable giving people tough but loving feedback.	1	2	3	4	5
I am good at keeping the peace.	1	2	3	4	5
I don't like giving feedback to people. I don't want to hurt their feelings.	1	2	3	4	5
Getting constructive feedback is uncomfortable. I am really hard on myself.	1	2	3	4	5
I appreciate getting constructive feedback; it helps me become a better educator/leader.	1	2	3	4	5
I am energized by conflict (not good or bad, just energized.)	1	2	3	4	5
I am good at setting boundaries and saying no with colleagues.	1	2	3	4	5
I am good at setting boundaries and saying no with my supervisor.	1	2	3	4	5
I am good at setting boundaries and saying no to youth.	1	2	3	4	5
I am comfortable naming my needs to others.	1	2	3	4	5

So, what did you learn about yourself? What *"aha!!"* moments did you have? How we engage in conflict depends on so many things: our identities, the identities of those we are in conflict with, the culture of the team or the broader school, our upbringings, and so much more. You may have reflected that you are good at setting boundaries and saying no *sometimes*; perhaps you are great at it with your family, but you struggle with this at work. You might have realized that you are very receptive to getting feedback from youth but getting feedback from your direct supervisor who has historically belittled you, is much harder.

Learning to Skillfully Navigate Conflict

Just as discussed in Chapter 2, no emotions are inherently good or bad. This sentiment is also true of conflict. Conflict itself is neither good nor bad. The *way* we express our emotions has the potential to create further harm, and the *ways* we engage in conflict can be destructive or generative.

Bill Warters of the Conflict Resolution Education Connection (2025) defines generative conflict as: "creating conflicts that are functional in order to enhance creativity and constructive change" (n.p.). Generative conflict creates opportunities for us to learn from each other and to make changes that are beneficial. Conflict is a powerful pathway toward deepening relationships and becoming more aligned with our integrity.

Destructive vs. Generative Conflict

Destructive conflict is about winning and not about developing mutual understanding. Destructive conflict often contains: insults, belittling comments, dismissal of dissenting perspectives especially around challenging policies and practices that are sustaining inequities, and personal attacks. This type of conflict is omnipresent in our news cycle and in the media broadly.

Generative conflict will not lead to everyone thinking and acting in the same way. Our values and our beliefs will always clash with other people. Generative conflict makes room for possibilities and potential for change but it doesn't guarantee a swift outcome.

Reactivity

In conflict, we may get incredibly reactive. Our reactivity is like a flashing warning sign that says "DANGER." However, with a flooded nervous system, we often ignore that sign and forge ahead anyway. Physiological reactivity may feel hot, tense, and rigid, or like a tea kettle that's been boiling for a long time. Examining your physiological cues of reactivity is incredibly helpful in knowing what is actually happening when you are in conflict.

You may not be someone who tends to go to the fight/flight response. That's okay; you can skip to the next section: evading conflict. For the people who tend to be more reactive, what does reactivity sound like? Feel like? How would you describe the physical sensations? Are you always aware that you are reactive in the moment or does it take some time for you to process what happened?

A workshop participant asked me what to do when the person you are in conflict with is clearly in a reactive state but doesn't believe themselves to be. My best answer is to use an "I" statement. Do not, I repeat, do not, tell the person that they are being reactive and that they need to calm down. Take a deep breath, or anything similar. It will amplify that person's rage. Instead you can try phrases like these:

- *I'm feeling really overwhelmed by this conversation. It's important to me that I can really listen to you and be receptive, so I am going to take 15 minutes to get myself together, and then I'll reconnect with you.*
- *I'm not in a great place to be reflective right now. I need to pause this for now, and I'll email/text/call you so we can schedule a time to come back to this.*

These phrases do a few things. They let the person know that you care about what they have to say and are committing to reconnecting with them in a certain timeframe. These phrases also focus on *you* rather than *them*, which can de-escalate tension.

Your sincerity matters. Even if you say these phrases perfectly, if you are just saying it to get out of the situation, they will know you are BS-ing them. Practicing these phrases across contexts and with different people will help this become more natural. I also suggest avoiding having a stock response. It will immediately be coded as insincere.

Evading Conflict

While we may not physically remove ourselves from a conflict, we may disappear ourselves. We may become silent or withdrawn. We may become passive-aggressive in an attempt to get our unspoken needs met. Sometimes the power dynamics within an organization amplify this conflict style. An authoritarian leadership that relies on a power-over, retaliation, and coercion style may increase the need for people to talk behind closed doors rather than address conflict directly. The fear of being publicly humiliated, shamed, ridiculed, or belittled causes people to talk about the issues between each other rather than find ways to talk with the person/people who need accountability. Evading conflict may show up as:

- People pleasing
- Conforming to the status quo, even though it feels wrong
- Talking behind people's backs
- Saying yes to someone, doing the thing, and feeling incredibly resentful
- Saying yes, and doing a mediocre job in hopes they won't ask you do to it again
- Trying to find quick solutions, such as "Say you're sorry," without addressing harm that has occurred

Reflecting on Your Conflict Styles

This is where returning to the practices in Chapter 3 on emotional awareness can support us in learning to embrace conflict as a pathway toward change.

1. When someone has let you know they are negatively impacted by your actions, what emotions come up for you?
2. What are some of your patterns of reactivity?
3. In what situations are you more likely to be reactive?
4. Are there people you are more reactive with?
5. In what situations are you likely to evade conflict?
6. Are there particular people that you evade conflict with?
7. Why do you think this happens?
8. How are your conflict patterns working for you?
9. When you are engaged in conflict with someone with a different conflict style, how does this impact you?

Note: Some people may have patterns of conflict that are disruptive and generate more harm, and they may be unwilling to self-reflect. You can't force them to, no matter how much you might want to try.

Conflict includes disagreement and relational disruption that often stem from misunderstandings or differing values that can be addressed through healthy dialogue. Conflict is very different from abuse, which is a pattern of repeated behavior intended to demean or control someone else's behavior. Abuse cannot be addressed through healthy dialogue and needs a different level of intervention.

Dissent as Healthy

Some people believe that when people express dissent and frustration that they are "being negative." The expression of frustration is not the source of "negativity." A hostile work environment and authoritarian leadership create and fuel negativity. Listening to people tell the truth of their experiences may be uncomfortable, challenging, and overwhelming for the people who have instituted the policies and practices. Similarly, receiving feedback about our teaching or lessons may be uncomfortable. However, discussing the impact is not creating negativity; it is an opportunity to change something that isn't working. Attempts to silence dissent will not eradicate the issue.

Many of us did not learn how to navigate discomfort in a functional way growing up. Rarely do we know how to engage in conflict with the goal of learning and transforming. The underlying intention often seems to be one of the following: destroy, win, or keep the peace. Approaching conflict with those hidden agendas leaves little room for us to change our patterns or transform our personal and professional lives.

Conflict with the Values of Other People

In Chapter 5, we explored values. Commonly, people believe that everyone working in education shares the same values. However, this is not the case. I often hear from people statements like, "Well, we're in education because we care about children." That may be true, but the ways people think about *care* differs immensely. My version of *care* may be connected to my values of compassion and adaptability, and my belief that we must continue to adapt and adjust how we are working with students and each other to ensure our schools are disrupting harm and creating safety. Another person's version of *care* might be connected to their values of discipline and self-reliance and their beliefs that students must learn how to follow rules in order to be successful in the world. Our values and beliefs will clash.

As mentioned in Chapter 5, our values can and do change. However, it is not a good use of our precious time and energy to try to dictate other people's values, even if we believe that will benefit students and families. Just as I do not imagine myself being swayed toward holding a core value around discipline, it is unlikely that I will sway someone else to move their core value to adaptability when it comes to how we support students. It is challenging, but combining radical acceptance (Brach, 2004; Linehan, 1993) along with a clear understanding of your values and ethics can allow you to focus your energy in places it is actually needed.

Radical acceptance is a practice in a form of cognitive behavioral therapy (Linehan, 1993) and is also found in Tara Brach's (2004) book, *Radical Acceptance*. The tenets are found in many secular mindfulness trainings and many other spiritual practices. The practice is to acknowledge what is true, recognize the suffering in yourself and others, and accept what is outside of your control. Accepting what *is* does not mean avoiding responsibility to influence change; it means you are not taking other people on as projects.

Reflection: Examining Your Organization

There are unspoken and unwritten rules for how conflict is handled within organizations and on teams. Take some time to reflect on these patterns. Consider setting an intention for a week or two of being an observer of conflict in various settings. If your work is primarily with other adults, the prompts below can be helpful.

- Within your organizations and/or teams, how is conflict generally addressed?
- How often is direct conflict part of your organizational/team culture?

- What does accountability look like within your organization and team?
- Within your organization and/or teams…
  - Whose perspectives are most centered in conflict?
  - Whose perspectives are most frequently disbelieved?
  - What patterns of racism, sexism, ableism, queerphobia, xenophobia, classism, etc. do you notice in your above responses?

If you work with both students and adults, the prompts below may be helpful in guiding your reflection:

- When two students are engaged in conflict, what do you usually do, or what do you observe adults most frequently doing?
  - Try to stop it immediately but tell them to stop?
  - Encourage a quick resolution—apologize and move on?
  - Ask if they need support in sorting it out?
  - Remind them of the tools and strategies they can use to engage in generative conflict?

What patterns did you notice? Do those patterns seem to be working to create space for *generative conflict?*

The Power of a Pause

As discussed in Chapter 3, our emotions are absolutely worthy of being fully heard and seen but not at the expense of other people. If you are in a mode of wanting to belittle someone, put someone in their place, or teach someone a lesson, that is something to take notice of and work toward making a different choice. If there is name-calling, blaming, monologuing, or other non-constructive patterns, the best thing we can do, and one of the most challenging things to do, is to pause.

Pausing and moving away from the place that has erupted into chaos creates room for the potential that deeper resolution will happen with less hurt. *But what about when someone dehumanizes me?* This is such an important question. No one is required to tolerate or pretend that a dehumanizing comment, whether intentional or not, does not deeply wound them. The question I ask back is "Does dehumanizing the other person help you?" Pausing and moving away does not mean brushing it off, moving past it, or any other form of compartmentalizing. It means giving ourselves and the other people some time to settle our nervous systems so we can create the possibility to engage in the hard work of accountability.

It is important to have plans in place and to practice taking pauses in a variety of settings with different people. Sometimes we try to implement a practice we have learned the theory of but haven't practiced and embodied and it fails miserably. Then we feel miserable and think "Well, that practice didn't work."

Building this into your ethos/community agreements can promote this practice in becoming habitual. There can be a communal understanding that when things start to become too heated, there is a mechanism to pause and to come back to the conflict after people are able to re-settle their nervous systems.

If you notice that something is going awry, work toward naming how *you* are experiencing the moment. It can be helpful to practice TONAL so that you can build awareness of what is happening for you. It is challenging, but when you are able to take ownership of your emotional response and name what you need in the moment, it shifts the energy in a room. This is co-regulation in action.

Imagine for a moment a meeting that is going badly. People are talking over each other. One person is on their laptop. Another person hasn't said anything for about 10 minutes and looks like they're going to cry. In this scenario, what do you usually do? Is your usual pattern helpful to the situation? If so, that's amazing. I have no notes! If you have a stress/overwhelm response that moves you toward an *immobility/freeze* response, what would be something different you could try? If you go into a *fight/flee* response, what is something different you could try? Here are some potential options:

Fight/Flee Response		
Habit	*Inner Shift*	*Outer Shift*
Make a passive aggressive remark "I thought we were all adults here"	T: tune in O: observe sensations and thoughts N: name the emotion and experience A*: allow the emotion to move L: loving response to self A*: *this might be subtly clenching and releasing your fists, rolling your feet and ankles, or tightening your body and releasing, or taking some slower, longer exhales. The release of tension is important for this response.*	"I'm frustrated with how this meeting is going. Can we refocus?"
Push your chair away from the table and leave		"I am annoyed that we are so distracted from the problem. I'd like to take a 5 minute break and come back and regroup."
Talk about how someone else is feeling. "Look what you're doing to poor Janine."		"This doesn't seem to be working. Can we take a minute to figure out how to address how we're talking to each other?"
Freeze Response		
Habit	*Inner Shift*	*Outer Shift*
Say nothing	T: tune in O: observe sensations and thoughts N: name the emotion and experience A*: allow the emotion to move L: loving response to self *A*: for a freeze response, bringing any kind of little movement, even if it's just wiggling your toes, can be helpful to not feel so stuck. Rocking in your chair, rubbing your fingertips together, moving your eyes to a different place in the room or looking out of a window if it's available. Bringing movement*	"I would like to take a short break."
Daydream		"I wonder if it might be helpful to look at our agenda again."
Stare at your computer screen or phone		"I noticed we are running over. Could we figure out what to do?"

It is important to remember that someone states with confidence and assertion "Hey, I think we're off track here" may be perfectly inwardly regulated. Their social identity and your biases may elicit a desire to tell them to "speak kinder." People with a *freeze response* may speak quieter and softer, but that doesn't mean their responses are "better" or more desirable than more direct responses. Let's revisit tone policing from Chapter 11 to understand how to avoid this unhelpful and harmful practice.

Tone policing focus on the *tone* with which someone is expressing themselves rather than the content. More examples of this will discussed later in the book. Our racialized and gendered biased perceptions of "anger" may result in *tone policing;* we may ask someone to "speak calmly" when they have the full right to be frustrated, irritated, displeased, etc. because of our own discomfort.

Reflecting on Tone Policing

Take a moment to center through any practice that will feel supportive. Then take some time to reflect on when you have experienced tone policing or have enacted tone policing. Notice how your body feels and the emotions that surface. What stories are you telling yourself about yourself? Are they helpful or shame-based?

If you were tone-policed and didn't say anything, how does that feel? What were the circumstances that made the environment psychologically or emotionally unsafe to push back?

If you tone-policed someone, how does that feel? What experiences of shame or guilt are surfacing? It may be helpful to revisit the shame avoidance strategies in Chapter 3. What would you like to do differently in the future?

Conflict Affirmations

These affirmations can support you in changing your relationship to conflict.

- There are times when it is not comfortable for me to speak up; that is a "system" issue not a "me" issue.
- There are times I have avoided conflict even when I could have spoken up; I can do something different now.
- Conflict is not a problem; it can help us to grow and change.
- Not every issue can be resolved through generative conflict.
- People have a right to be upset at injustice; I do not need to stifle their reasonable emotions even if I am uncomfortable.

CHAPTER SUMMARY

Engaging in generative conflict creates opportunities for us for our practices, curricula, pedagogies, and beliefs to be challenged and changed. Changework can only be sustained if we are committed to learning how to move away from destructive conflict toward generative conflict centered on hope, healing, and justice. A statement on the header of a meeting agenda that "we have psychological safety" is not enough. There must be matching actions and inactions that co-create this type of interpersonal safety.

13

Relational Repair Work

Relational Repair Work

The conflation of causing harm with being a "bad person" prevents far too many people from engaging in true accountability and self-reflective work. As we explored in the previous chapter, many of our school/school system cultures are conflict avoidance or engage in destructive conflict rather than generative conflict. We also must understand our own relationship to conflict in order to be courageous enough to participate in accountability processes. Accountability is not punishment. It is not social rejection through detention or other forms of social exclusion, including workplace bullying and gossip; nor is it shame-based. It is a process in which the humanity of everyone involved is at the center while ensuring we are addressing power imbalances.

Accountability

Mia Mingus, in her 2019 online piece "The Four Parts of Accountability & How To Give A Genuine Apology," gives us these reminders:

> We will hurt, misunderstand, and harm each other. We are human and we live in an incredibly violent and harmful world. The point is to learn how to be accountable when we inevitably mess up, so that we know what to

DOI: 10.4324/9781003540687-14

> do. This is not to let anyone off the hook or excuse or justify harm. Instead, this is a push for us to acknowledge the reality of harm, rather than continue to live in the fantasies we've created about harm. We will all mess up and make terrible mistakes. We will all hurt people we love and care about at some point. We will all have our time on the chopping block. We want to try and reduce harm whenever we can and that is different than trying to avoid conflict or pretend away hurt.
>
> *(n.p.)*

When we have been harmed, relational repair work invites us to be honest with ourselves and honest with others.

In *The Politics of Trauma*, Staci K. Haines (2019) describes the ways in which we may skirt and avoid accountability when we experience shame. She describes this as "under-accountability," which is:

> avoidance of, dodging, deflecting, or denying accountability…later we may feel ashamed, guilty, or see our part, yet not take action to be accountable. Instead, we may hide our sense of shame and "move on". We are under-accountable when we avoid affecting things within our spheres of influence, or don't face mistakes and impacts we have had with good intent and responsibility.
>
> *(p. 310)*

Oftentimes people with socially dominant identities are socialized to be *under-accountable* and people with societally marginalized identities are socialized and pressured to be *over-accountable*.

Accountability is a process and a gift we give ourselves and those we are in community with. It is a practice of being self-aware enough that we are responsible for ourselves. Throughout this book, there have been invitations for you to reflect on your values and your *intention–action gaps*. We are self-responsible in the moments we recognize the distance between our values and work toward shrinking that distance. Accountability also happens when we realize the hurt or harm we have caused to someone else or others and we address the hurt directly and respect the needs of the person who was hurt.

Defensive maneuvers are intended to keep us from experiencing discomfort. They are sometimes subconscious and sometimes intentional. Habitually avoiding the discomfort of accountability prevents us from growing and changing. When we need to be accountable, we can tend to our discomfort through self-compassion.

Radical Self-Compassion

While it may feel selfish to engage in self-compassion, it is actually helpful in alleviating some of the intensity of shame and guilt so that we can move out of those emotions and into reparative action or changed behavior. Dr. Kristin Neff is a self-compassion researcher and her website offers descriptions of the three elements of self-compassion.

The first element is Self-kindness vs. Self-judgment. She describes how people who are "self-compassionate" can "recognize that being imperfect, failing, and experiencing life difficulties is inevitable" and therefore "tend to be gentle with themselves when confronted with painful experiences rather than getting angry when life falls short of set ideals."

The second element is Common humanity vs. Isolation. This component emphasizes the understanding "that suffering and personal inadequacy is part of the shared human experience – something that we all go through rather than being something that happens to 'me' alone".

The third element is Mindfulness vs. Over-identification. Neff writes that "Mindfulness is a non-judgmental, receptive mind state in which one observes thoughts and feelings as they are, without trying to suppress or deny them.". This is in contrast to over-identification in which one can get stuck or "caught up" in negative feelings. Each of these components supports the other. Below is an example of an interaction that may happen and how using self-compassion can support moving out of a shame spiral.

A family member calls you and says "I am concerned that you do not like Romero. He is the only Latine student in the classroom and he is constantly feeling targeted. I want to understand what is happening.". You immediately start to cry. You say "That's not true, I really do care about him. I would never do anything to hurt him." The family member says "Are you calling Romero a liar? He has never lied in his life." You say "No, I just can't understand why he would think that." The family member says "This was a waste of my time," and hangs up. You are shaken and confused.

This is a sample process for using self-compassion.

1. *Self-kindness vs. Self-judgment*: I am feeling overwhelmed by that conversation. I felt hurt and distressed. It is okay to feel those things.
2. *Community humanity vs. isolation*: Being taken by surprise is normal. I'm sure a lot of people would have reacted that way.
3. *Mindfulness vs. Over-identification*: I am feeling upset now, but I won't always feel upset.

This practice of self-soothing is powerful. Yet, it can inadvertently disallow us from reflecting on what we could have done differently. We need additional justice-centered contemplative skills to move us toward genuine repair.

After moving through the self-compassion practice, we also need to: a) reflect on power dynamics; b) differentiate harm from discomfort; and c) establish accountability through repair and changed behavior. We need radical self-compassion. This is how radical self-compassion would change the response above and catalyze change and accountability.

1. *Power dynamics*: I am White and my Latine student is feeling like I don't like him. He is the only Latine and migrant student in my class.

2. *Differentiate harm from discomfort*: Their family member wasn't calling me to be cruel. They didn't say anything harmful. I felt uncomfortable, but that discomfort is important for me to experience here.
3. *Accountability*: I will call the family member back, apologize for my defensive response, ask them more questions, and see if they want to come in with Romero so the three of us can talk about how I can show up in a more supportive way for him.

Radical self-compassion helps us become more acutely aware of power differences, our biases, and our personal responsibilities as we engage in repair work and accountability.

Differentiating Power Dynamics and Anger Origins

Anger is a potent and powerful emotion. The origins of anger are not singular; we need to become attuned to the very different reasons people experience and display anger. In Chapter 2, we discussed different shame-avoidance strategies including *moving against* (Brown, 2018; Hartling et al., 2000). In this strategy, people may become defensive, hostile, or belligerent. This sometimes happens in processes of accountability, especially those connected to issues of identity-based harm. Self-protective shame avoidance is incompatible with engaging in accountability. It might sound like "How dare you say that was racist. I am not racist." There is a critical distinction between this form of anger and the anger of defending oneself against dehumanization.

There is a very reasonable anger that originates from experiencing dehumanization. Social exclusion, bullying, harassment, and microaggression are all forms of dehumanization. To dehumanize is to deem someone unworthy. A rageful response is healthy. However, as we explored in Chapter 9, our perceptions of anger and the way we respond differs depending on *who* is expressing the anger. In a culture organized around whiteness and maleness as "normal" and "worthy," this often means White men and boys can engage in self-protective shame avoidance and evade accountability while the justified anger of Black youth in particular, and all people with societally marginalized identities, is dismissed, controlled, and policed. This can also be true for anyone of any racial identity naming and disrupting inequities, such as when a White person tries to address racism or other forms of oppression, and other White people become defensive and shift blame and focus onto the person naming the issue as being *the* problem. It is essential to continuously differentiate discomfort from harm; especially around issues of inequity and oppression.

Before you engage in repair work, it is essential to be conscientious of who has the power in a situation, the origins of the anger, and the social biases present. It has always been unreasonable to hold the person harmed for their reaction to a higher level of accountability than the person who harmed them. This exacerbates the harm cycle and prevents healing for all involved. Each person or persons involved in a repair process need healing. Their processes may be quite different. Staci K. Haines (2019) wrote in *The Politics of Trauma*:

> Those harmed need healing, agency, and structural power. And those who enact harm need transformation so as to shift from domination to equity, to take ongoing actions to rebuild trust, to demonstrate trustworthiness. At the level of systemic trauma, with which more personal traumas are interconnected, this requires both individual and collective healing, as well as structural change, both social and economic. These become inseparable for truly transforming trauma, and minimizing further trauma.
>
> *(p. 84)*

Repairing a harm or a hurt is rarely a simple or linear process. This process is much slower than the usual responses available in schools and school systems. We need slower responses to harm. Slower responses to harm allow us to uncover what is possible and what is not possible.

There may be times when an adult within the system is unable or unwilling to take responsibility for their actions, even with intervention and education. If this is true, tough decisions will need to be made. However, with youth, we as educators are responsible for finding as many paths toward repair as we can. Punishment and exclusion practices such as detention and suspensions do harm to our students. If we have exhausted our resources, we may need to tag someone else in or consult with outside agencies. Collaborative and healthy relationships with the family is essential in this repair work.

Preparing for Repair: Questions to Consider

It is highly recommended to work with a skilled facilitator with experience with trauma-informed and social justice work to support this process. Note that this process below can be used to identify if repair is possible. It is important to remember that repair is not always a possibility, especially in situations where one person or a group of people is completely unwilling to acknowledge they have caused harm. Below is a process for preparing for repair work and determining if repair is possible or not.

1. Has harm been differentiated from discomfort? If so, who has been harmed?
    a. Do they want to engage in a repair process?
    b. Is the harm ongoing?
        i. If so, repair is not recommended. Intervention and education with the person(s) responsible for harm is the first step.
2. Who has responsibility for the harm?
    a. Have they acknowledged they have responsibility?
        i. If no, repair is not recommended. Intervention and education with the person(s) responsible for harm is the first step.
3. Have power imbalances, both identity-based and positional, been clearly identified?
4. How might the power imbalances prevent someone/people from showing up authentically?

5. Are plans in place to take a pause if someone feels overwhelmed and needs to pause the discussion?
6. Have we identified the intention and purpose of the repair process?
   a. Is it clearly defined and agreed upon by everyone?
7. Are there mutually agreed-upon dialogue structures in place?
8. Have we ensured that the person harmed can express strong emotions without being asked to "relax" or "take a deep breath"? Note: *This may mean each party needs time and space to process those strong emotions with other people/in other spaces prior to reconvening.*
9. Do we have agreements on how we will engage in this dialogue?
10. Are alternative solutions needed such as using supervision or a restorative process?
11. Are interpreters and/or cultural liaisons invited to help facilitate cross-cultural conflict?

Moving Through Repair

Once the above has been co-created and there are mutually agreed-upon ways of sharing space, the process will unfold in this order: a) the person harmed/hurt communicates their hurt; b) the person receiving the story practices deep listening and self-soothing; c) the person receiving the story communicates understanding through an empathetic response; d) the person harmed/hurt offers ideas on repair; e) the two people collaboratively work toward a repair plan.

Communicating Hurt

A script may be as follows: "When you (action/words), I felt (feeling words)." This focuses on the *thing* that happened and how that *thing* impacted you. It may feel very cathartic and desirable to unleash all your frustrations on this person(people) and tell them exactly what kind of person you think they are. While that may feel good temporarily, it does not result in the kind of space needed for people to reflect and ultimately change how they are showing up in the world. The conversation below would be between colleagues and/or someone with whom you have a close relationship; not students.

> **This:** "I feel frustrated when I share my stress with you, that the responses I get are: *it's not that bad* or *I mean, you could try to be more positive*. Those responses feel dismissive I don't trust that my stress will be taken seriously by you.
>
> **Not this:** "You never listen. You're so unempathetic. It's like you don't even care about what I'm saying. I think you're just too self-centered to really listen".

The "this" is specific, tells the person how their responses impact you, and creates room for change. The "not this" has personal attacks (which may feel entirely true to you which is valid) but does not create opportunity for change. Both will create discomfort. The "this" is likely to be uncomfortable for both the sender and the recipient because it is vulnerable. To reiterate from above, this is specific to issues of conflict and not of abuse. There are times when a third party is recommended to help facilitate dialogue and to help identify barriers for healthy engagement in generative conflict if it seems people are stuck in the same conflict cycle.

Receiving the Story: Deep Listening and Embracing Discomfort

When we have caused harm – either intentionally or unintentionally – we need to be willing to openly hear the ways our actions, words, inactions, lack of words have impacted others. We also need to allow the person(s) harmed to tell us what they hope for and need.

In the moments when someone is sharing a hurt with us, either that we are responsible for or that someone else is responsible for, we may experience overwhelming emotions. Kazu Haga, a Kingian Nonviolence Facilitator, wrote that we can face violence, in its many forms, by "genuinely listening" to someone "when they are upset, hearing their pain, and taking full accountability for your actions without blaming or getting defense" (p. 41, 2020).

Deep listening (from Chapter 2) is a powerful practice to use when listening to someone share their hurt. While listening, it may be necessary to practice some self-soothing so that we are able to stay present and not escape behind one of our *shame avoidance* or other emotional avoidance strategies.

Self-Soothing

Actively soothing our nervous system communicates to the other person that there is emotional safety present and they will be able to share their hurt with you more authentically. Developing a strong TONAL practice with sticky emotions can build our capacity to receive uncomfortable, but necessary feedback.

Communicate Understanding with an Empathetic Response

This is the chart from Chapter 9, based on the work of Theresa Wiseman (1996), and is the process for providing an empathetic response to someone who has shared a hurt with us.

Four Elements of Empathy adapted from Wiseman, 1996.

Perspective: Take someone's perspective as their truth. Be willing to understand their story and perspective of events. You may not agree but you are willing to recognize their truth as their truth.	**Recognize & Disrupt Internal Judgment**: Notice your own patterns of judgment, bias, and assumptions. Label them as they show up and then invite them to take a rest.
Recognize & Understand the Person's Emotions/Feelings: Experience another person's feelings with them. Notice the difference between their feelings and your feelings in response to their feelings.	**Communicate Your Understanding of Their Feelings**: Acknowledge their feelings and validate that their feelings make sense, are legitimate, and reasonable.

Collaborative Repair

The closing part of the repair process is a collaborative development for repair. The *golden rule* implies that we should treat others the way we want to be treated. However, we are accountable to others when we employ the *platinum rule*, a phrase coined by Dr. Tony Alessandra and Michael O'Connor (1996). With the *platinum rule*, we treat others how they wish to be treated rather than presuming everyone wishes to be treated the way we are treated. This is a must for culturally-responsive and culturally-sustaining pedagogies and practices (Dhaliwal, 2016; Howard et al., 2020; Ladson-Billings, 2021). The *platinum rule* is in direct opposition to *saviorism*; the belief that those with power know what is best for others. With the *platinum rule*, we ask people and/or communities what they need and believe them rather than assuming to know what they need or correcting their requests. We can ask questions like:

1. What would be helpful for you to know that I understand the hurt?
2. How can I make this up to you?
3. What would show you that I am changing my behavior?

The person might ask for a 10-page essay about your reflections. You can respond with "I understand that a written reflection could be helpful. I will write something for you about what I learned and how I will be accountable, but it probably won't be 10 pages." This is an imperfect but genuine repair.

What to Watch Out For

As with anything, the language of emotions and repair processes can be weaponized. It is important to always center power differentials and to understand the ways defensive maneuvers present themselves. Overwhelmed nervous systems are not able to be in a repair process. Using the pause strategies from the previous chapter is, at times, necessary. We also need to be aware of how emotions and the language of emotions can be weaponized.

Weaponizing Emotions

As with everything, emotional expression can inadvertently be used as a way to detour discomfort. There are very skillful and adaptive ways people can weaponize the language and communication of their emotions to avoid conversations or emotions they feel uncomfortable with. This can sound like "Well, I just prefer to focus on the positive." In a team meeting, I shared that I was feeling "overwhelmed and stressed," and one of my colleagues immediately responded with "So, you're feeling busy." I said no, and restated my chosen words. She then said "Well, busy just has a more positive connotation." In addition to being overwhelmed and stressed, I was also livid because of her dismissive and attempt to correct my emotional language because she was uncomfortable with it. It is not our job to "correct" or offer replacement words to someone sharing their emotions.

Weaponizing emotions also pops up when there are conversations about statements that have led to social harm. This is particularly true when people of the Global Majority and people whose identities have been societally marginalized are expressing their anger as discussed in Chapter 9. As mentioned earlier in this chapter, this can also happen to people with dominant racial identities working to disrupt injustices. For example, if someone brings up discriminatory practices in a school related to dress code and/or hair styles, people may use emotional language to try to turn the focus to the person naming the harm or hurt, such as "It makes me sad you would think we're the type of people to be discriminatory." This is weaponizing emotions to avoid accountability. This is present in *tone policing* as well. This prevents necessary discussions and change from happening and perpetuates the issues.

People must learn to take responsibility for their discomfort when being asked to examine issues of justice and equity, and they must learn how to sit with the discomfort of experiencing guilt and/or shame. Exploring, understanding, and processing our emotions with others is necessary, especially if we are in distress. However, we need to learn the boundaries of emotional expression as well as the alluring nature of weaponizing our emotions. Here are some examples of emotional weaponization:

- *A non-disabled educator tells a disabled student "It makes me feel sad when you don't follow my directions."*
- *A principal, a White Woman, tells a Black parent of a Black fourth grader, whom the administrator recently sent home for*

"dress code violations:" "I am hurt that you would think I treat your child any differently because of the color of their skin" and begins to cry.

- *A middle-aged White man, a classroom teacher tells a Southeast Asian woman, an interventionist in his classroom, "You know, it would make me feel better if you brought a more positive attitude into the classroom. I felt uncomfortable when you weren't laughing at my jokes."*

In each of these examples, there are power dynamics of social location (position within an organization and hierarchy) and of social identity.

In the first example, a non-disabled educator is creating a situation in which a disabled student is responsible forthe emotional wellness of the adult and is setting up the student to feel guilt or shame when they are "making" this educator "sad." This interaction is coercing a student to follow directions and to comply. A better response from this educator would be "I'm feeling frustrated right now. and I need a couple of minutes to sit with my feelings." Then, they can ask the student about their experience and get curious about why the student might be struggling to follow directions. As the educator, it is our responsibility to sit with our own emotions, process them, and to get to a place where we can ask the student what we need, rather than ask the student to center our needs.

The second example is a case of the White administrator centering their own hurt feelings, rather than acknowledging and addressing the Black parent's perspective of anti-Blackness as a factor in their young child being sent home from school. This creates a scenario in which the parent is stuck. They can *soothe* and *console* the White administrator, while simultaneously suppressing their anger at the initial injustice and the additional experience of being told race isn't a factor. The other option is to openly express their frustration and be at risk of being labeled as threatening. Neither option is tenable. The White administrator, instead, needs to feel their own feelings (guilt, shame, fear, anxiety, etc.) and be receptive to what families of color are saying about their experiences. A better response would be "Thank you for bringing this to my attention, I really do need to examine my own biases. In the meantime, please accept my apology and I will also apologize to your child." There is a very important distinction between feeling emotional and using one's tears to avoid and evade accountability. There are ample resources online and in books that further unpack of the ways White women's tears have been utilized resulting in harm to the Black community, and to racial justice efforts broadly. I strongly encourage you to read more about this.

The third example is a case of a man asking a woman to perform *emotional labor* so that he feels better. She may not think his humor is funny, and may even find it offensive at times. She is under no obligation to perform finding someone funny for anyone at any time. A better response from the classroom teacher would be to engage in some self-reflection on why he feels that he is owed her attention and her laughter. He could also ask, and be receptive to her response without being defensive, "I noticed you don't laugh much at the jokes I make. Can I ask why?" In this scenario, she is entirely welcome to say "I'll get back to you about that," or "Let's talk another time." Likely, their relationship could benefit from rebalancing power and rebuilding trust before she will be and feel safe enough to give an honest answer without fear of retribution.

Non-Weaponization of Emotions and Empathy

In the above "redo" examples, there are some hints of *how* to express your emotions in a way that does not make someone else responsible for your emotions.

The formula is: a thing that a person did/is doing that caused harm had this emotional impact on me. The formula in weaponization of emotions is: you called my attention to something I said or did that was hurtful or harmful, and now you need to take care of my hurt feelings. Telling someone how their hurtful or harmful actions impacted you is incredibly brave and vulnerable.

Pause and Reflect

Take a moment to pause and reflect on how your body feels and the emotions surfacing as you finish this chapter. Your identities and life experiences influenced how it felt to read this chapter. What are some ways you want to embody accountability? What are some ways you have avoided accountability in the past?

Accountability Affirmations

- This person is deserving of love and care.
- It is a gift when someone trusts me and shares with me how I have hurt them.
- It takes courage to mend hurt.
- It takes courage to tell someone they have hurt me.
- I deserve repair.
- I can learn to differentiate between harm and discomfort.
- Discomfort does not mean dysfunction; I can learn to navigate repair work with love.
- I don't have to repair with everyone. Sometimes a relationship cannot be mended.
- It is important to remember who has *power* in a situation.
- Accountability is a gift.

CHAPTER SUMMARY

Accountability is a process in which we take responsibility for ourselves and repair hurt and harm. Our social locations and social identities influence our relationship to *under-* and *over-accountability*. Practicing self-soothing can support us in creating an opportunity for someone to share their hurt without being worried we will be defensive or move away from accountability. Sharing our hurt in a way that doesn't shame or blame someone else takes practice and is helpful. Hearing someone's hurt does not mean we are being shamed or blamed.

14

We Are the Changemakers

We Are the Changemakers

Change does not occur without you or without us. We are the changemakers. The diagram below represents the interconnection between oneself, others, and the world. We are influenced by others, we influence others, we are influenced by the world, and we influence the world. Others are influenced by the world and the world influences other people. This is an ongoing cycle.

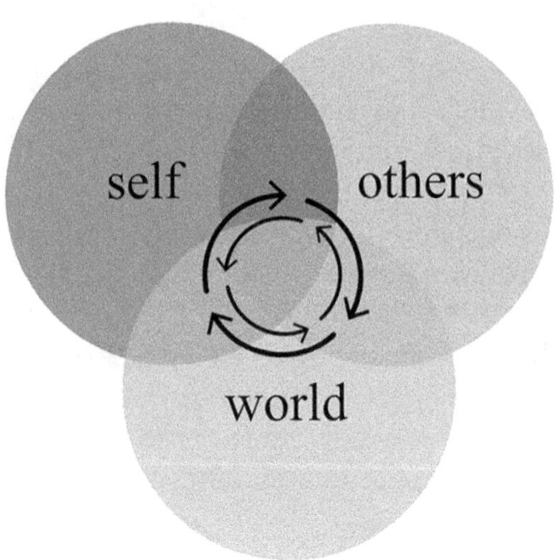

FIGURE 14.1 Cycles of Influence

DOI: 10.4324/9781003540687-15

One of my favorite Thich Nhat Hanh quotes is "We are here to awaken from the illusion of our separateness." We are not alone on this journey, and that feeling of aloneness and sense of separation from others leads to making decisions that may be temporarily good for the self but not the many. This is present at the large scale, such as billionaires resource hoarding, and at the small scale, when someone unilaterally makes a decision on behalf of a group of people (e.g. choosing a curriculum or when students are disallowed from moving their bodies during long instruction because it is challenging for the teacher.

In his book *How to Fight* he writes

> Interbeing is the understanding that nothing exists separately from anything else. We are all interconnected. By taking care of another person, you take care of yourself. By taking care of yourself, you take care of the other person. Happiness and safety are not individual matters.
>
> *(Hanh, 2017)*

Every day you are directly influencing our world and other people. The choices you make create opportunities to support healing, wholeness, and collaboration or to maintain the status quo.

Using the Intention–Action Gap to Facilitate Change

Throughout this book, there have been invitations to examine your own intention–action gaps and your school/school system intention–action gaps. Our personal values are to lead or teach with compassion, yet we realize that our level of burnout has left us little room to extend compassion to ourselves or others. These gaps are opportunities to engage in generative conflict to ignite and incite change. This is where radical self-compassion and collaborative partnerships are essential in addressing our individual intention-action gaps and in identifying and addressing organizational intention-action gaps.

Organizational Intention–Action Gaps

Organizational intention-action gaps might include a school promoting the value of equity while allowing some educators to remove LGBTQIA+ history and books. It is also when a school system highlights their dedication and commitment to gender equality, yet cisgender boys are still disproportionately enacting violence against cisgender girls and LGBTQIA+ students. A colleague and I co-created content for an anti-racist professional development series. One of the sessions was about accountability versus punishment. We wrote a piece that highlighted research that points out that educators are more likely to rely on implicit biases and inadvertently cause harm. One participant left anonymous feedback and wrote the following:

> The article was almost offensive, especially at the elementary level. The thought that those adults we work closely with "have hurt or harmed students," based on their own stress is mind boggling. We work SO HARD with all of our kids and do everything possible to check our bias and focus on anti-racist practices. Having to read an article that states the educators that we know and love are harming students based on our own stress or not being accountable for ourselves is truly disheartening.

There were a couple of other respondents who shared that the article felt "disrespectful." There were far more educators who did not share this sentiment. The majority of responses reflected that this content was important, as it reflected what they saw as the reality of working in education. Multiple truths coexist. Educators absolutely work hard every single day and educators work in a system that was not designed to be equitable. Educators have worked toward disrupting inequities, and our schools are not equitable.

Nearly every data point in the school system from this example said exactly what our mini-article was highlighting; students of the Global Majority were not reaching their full academic potential, and if you were Black, experiencing poverty, and/or served by an Individualized Education Plan, you were significantly more likely to be suspended. The data also showed that LGBTQIA+

students were more likely to experience bullying and harassment. It is not tenable to pretend that the data only reflect the influences of the individual students, their families, and the "outside world." We have to build the courage to be honest about what happens in our schools every day that creates these data patterns.

There are data points in your school or workplace that are indications of where the intention and action gap is happening systemically. Consider the following prompts to assess intention–action gaps at your organization.

- Does your team, school, or educational organization have a mission statement or other values-driven statements?
  - According to those statements, what are the values of the group?
    - Are those values similar to, or different from, your core values?
    - In what ways?
    - How does this feel for you?
- In what ways is the group (team, school, educational organization) living up to their values?
- In what ways is the group not living up to their values?
- How do you feel about this?

Revisit your earlier responses in this chapter about the current climate and culture to see what your school culture is organized around. If your school culture is organized around overworking and self-sacrifice, what would be helpful changes within the culture? These changes will take time. These suggestions need support from formal leadership positions.

As Ruth King reminds us that "Without wise awareness, habitual patterns rule our lives…in this potent pause [with mindfulness practice], we can ask, *is how I am thinking and feeling contributing to suffering or to freedom*" (2018). Mike Murawski (2020) offered these powerful questions that I invite you to consider.

- What is my work to become a better human?
- What is my own power and privilege within society and within the structures of this institution?
- In what ways have I been making decisions based on the norms and expectations of a toxic workplace culture?

- How am I complicit in creating or reinforcing the conditions of a toxic work culture?
- How can I break free from existing and traditional expectations, and lead from my heart and from a place of humanness – despite the risks or consequences?

Take 5–15 minutes to journal or reflect silently on the above prompts. Notice what it feels like to reflect on your own contributions to the overall culture and climate. Be curious toward any emotional responses that are surfacing. Practice TONAL: *Tune in, Observe sensations & thoughts, Name the emotion and experience, Allow the emotion to move, Loving response to self* as you move through your emotions. Try not to suppress or otherwise avoid any discomfort. What does it feel like to think about and dream about ways to shift the climate and culture?

Our Wellness Is Not Optional

In the first chapter, we discussed how foundational mindfulness practices, while helpful, will not, on their own, create systemic change. Far too often, people are expected to do more with an over-emphasis on "self-care," rather than acknowledging and addressing the cultural and systemic issues that are causing harm.

When a school or school system is organized around urgency ("This has to get done yesterday"), scarcity ("There isn't enough time"), competition ("The other class is doing better than your class"), and perfectionism ("Everything must be done perfectly and I must be perfect"), this has a detrimental impact on everyone in the system. Educator stress directly impacts their own well-being and student well-being. Taking wellness within schools and school systems seriously is not optional. We must take our own wellness seriously, even when the systems around us do not promote or encourage it. We need rest, loving boundaries, hope, and joy.

Prioritizing Rest

In her 2022 book *Rest is Resistance: A Manifesto*, Tricia Hersey wrote "all of culture is working in collaboration for us to not rest, and when we do listen to our bodies and take rest, many feel extreme guilt and shame" (p. 17). Experiencing identity-based trauma (e.g. racial trauma), working toward justice in schools, combined with the stress of working in schools/school systems is a "perfect storm" contributing to sleep deprivation (Hirshberg et al., 2023; Pizarro & Kohli, 2020; Saleem et al., 2020). The impact of sleep deprivation cannot be understated. According to Johns Hopkins Medicine (2025), sleep deprivation over the long term can contribute to diabetes, depression, high blood pressure, stroke, and heart disease (n.p.). Sleep deprivation can also reduce our cognitive capacity and emotional regulation skills. Our short-term memory and attention suffer and there is a decrease in our ability to navigate high-intensity emotions skillfully (Cao et al., 2025; Krause et al., 2017). We must prioritize and take our sleep health seriously. Not using screens 1-2 hours before bed and dimming lights before bed are two simple ways to start.

Hersey (2022) reminds us in her work that *rest* does not mean sleep. Rest can mean using some of the foundational mindfulness practices, sitting in a chair and gazing out the window for 5 minutes, or closing our eyes and just being. If you are someone who says "Yes, well I prefer to rest by being active," that is not resting; it is avoiding rest. Resting means you are fully allowing your body to settle and relax. It means you are not multitasking or thinking about your to-do list.

Take a moment to recall the last time you rested during your day. What does rest feel like in your body? Can you access the sensation of restfulness? What is a practice or a place that helps you access restfulness? What distractions keep you from engaging in restfulness (e.g. social media, 24/7 news cycle, TV, podcasts, etc.)? What is one practice you can commit to embedding into your days that is intentionally restful?

Depending on your life, finding moments to rest may be very difficult. Caring for others in your home, such as newborns, infants, and/or elders, may decrease the access you have for time to yourself. Even if you can take 5 minutes while you're riding public transportation to take in the scenery and let your body soften, or 5 minutes in the car before you go inside, that can make a world of difference.

Setting Boundaries from Love with Love

Far too many of us have been taught through societal expectations and norms and cultural norms that setting boundaries is selfish. It is not. It is important to be aware of what you will and will not tolerate in terms of unreasonable and unhealthy work expectations. Boundaries are a way to protect our precious energy. They are not walls, and they do not dictate what other people do. Boundaries are not meant to be rigid. There will be times when we must flex and shift our boundaries around bringing work home or staying late. It is important we are clear on *why* we are adjusting our boundary and that it is not coming from a place of self-sacrifice so that we are not later resentful. If we say *yes* when we mean *no* to social or workplace pressure (if your job is not on the line), we are the ones responsible for that resentment.

Setting boundaries is an act of love toward ourselves. It may not seem like it, but it is also an act of love to our broader community. Demonstrating that boundaries are possible to set from love and sent with love is powerful.

Below are examples of non-boundaries, internal boundaries, and external boundaries. The non-boundaries are controlling other people and sidelining growth and accountability. The internal boundaries are examples of messages for yourself about what you are and are not willing to tolerate or be responsible for. The third column is ideas on how to communicate those boundaries to others.

Not a Boundary	*Internal Boundary*	*Communicating the Boundary*
People just need to deal with who I am. If they don't like me they can deal with it.	I am aware I am not perfect. I am open to meaningful feedback, but I will not tolerate being ridiculed or put down. I will also not have my identities disparaged. I will stand up against that.	*"I will not tolerate being insulted. If it continues, I will leave this space".*
You have to stop asking me to do everything. Don't you know I already have enough on my plate?	I do not need to adjust myself to people's unrealistic expectations of me. I say *no* when I do not have the time, energy, or bandwidth to give more.	*"I wish I could, but I don't have the bandwidth to volunteer for this event."*
Your emotions are not my responsibility.	I am not responsible for people's emotions but I am responsible for how I impact other people.	*"I stand by my choice to surface issues of inequities in our school. I won't apologize for the discomfort is surfaced."*
Don't email me after work hours.	I need quality time with people I love, so I do not check my work email after 4 p.m.	*"I do not check my work email after 4 p.m. or on the weekends."*

Take note any worries you may have about upsetting people. Even when we set boundaries from love with love, people may have strong reactions, but overextending ourselves and perpetually people pleasing is unsustainable. As you explore setting boundaries, find ways to communicate them that are authentic to you. You can try using some mini-practices and then practice saying your boundaries aloud from a firm, centered place. Take note of what it feels like to share your boundaries from love with love.

Practicing & Embodying Hope

We need hope. We are in desperate need of powerful and potent hope to address the myriad issues we are experiencing daily. We need people who feel this hope so intensely that they move us out of beliefs and practices that keep people stuck and toward ways of being in community with each other that help us heal, grow, and be whole.

Take a moment to reflect on the last time you felt hope. In mindfulness practices, there is a key component of *non-attachment*. This is helpful in releasing our often tight grip around our expectations connected to perfectionism. Hope is not "I hope my lesson plan goes perfectly." Nothing will ever be perfect, including ourselves. Hope is the energy of knowing that something better and different is possible.

bell hooks, author, educator, and social activist, powerfully noted that "hope is essential to any political struggle for radical change when the overall social climate promotes disillusionment and despair." There are many reasons for us to feel despair, yet we need hope to move us. Mariame Kaba, organizer, educator, archivist, and curator, highlights the power of hope:

> It's work to be hopeful. It's not like a fuzzy feeling. Like, you have to actually put in energy, time, and you have to be clear-eyed, and you have to hold fast to having a vision. It's a hard thing to maintain. But it matters to have it, to believe that it's possible, to change the world.

In schools, with the fast pace and the pressure to perform and conform to standardized assessments and prepackaged educational programs, it can seem like there is no room for hope. Yet, there are educators, who continue to find ways to use their hope to disrupt and push back against harmful educational practices every single day. Without hope, we may become hopeless, aimless, and complacent.

Take a moment to think about *hope*. If you can't access that emotion, think about someone you know or even someone you don't know who has embodied hope. It can be from a movie or an activist or a dear friend. Tap into that experience of hope. What does it feel like in your body? What would it feel like to access hope more often?

Embodying & Creating Room for Joy

Joy is such a needed emotional experience. In the 15+ years I have worked in education, I can only recall a handful of times when I witnessed joy being expressed in schools. Joy shows up as broad smiles, full uncontrollable belly laughs, hands clapping, rocking or folding over while laughing, knees being slapped, and hearts being full.

In your school/workplace, when was the last time you experienced joy? When was the last time you saw other people express joy? If you were expressing joy or seeing joy, what were other people's responses? To some, joy can seem dangerous. It is in direct opposition to the stifling systems that promote control.

Take some time to reflect on moments that have brought joy into your life. What does joy feel like to you? What sensations do you experience? What thoughts do you have? When was the last time you intentionally created room for joy or practiced joy? Dancing, singing, playing a game (and truly playing for the sake of playing not to win), watching something funny over and over again, being silly with a child or youth, being silly with other adults with whom you feel a sense of safety and ease. We can and must practice joy every chance we get.

Spheres of Influence

We can sometimes feel *powerless*. Burnout, moral injury, trauma, trauma exposure response and overwhelm and working with enormous systems organized around *power over* can increase our sense of powerlessness. It is imperative that we remember we do have power. This remembering instills hope within us and moves us toward change. Reflecting on what we do have control over and what we can directly influence can move us into thoughtful action.

The practice of reflecting on our spheres of influence (Covey, 2020) can help us sift through the noise of societal pressures and expectations to do everything we can, all the time. The following practice is an invitation to find clearer paths toward what you can directly influence which in turn, can alleviate the sense of overwhelming pressure that one person should be able to "do it all".

Reflecting on Spheres of Care, Influence & Control

For this reflection, we will consider our spheres of *care, influence,* and control. I suggest taking about 10–15 minutes for this reflection. Before you start, take some time to use a mindfulness

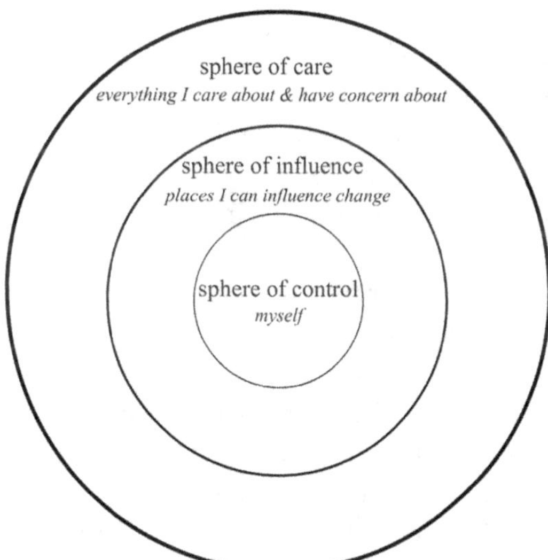

FIGURE 14.2 Spheres of Care, Influence, and Control

practice or any other practice to prepare your mind, body and heart.

Take some time to list all of the areas of *care* connected to changing your school, school system, and the external influences such as the political landscape, climate change, etc. Take as much time as you need with this. After you have written the list, notice how this feels. How does your body feel? What emotions are surfacing?

Then write all of the places you have influence over. It might be helpful to revisit your reflection on where you hold power within the system in Chapter 7 for this part. Now, notice how your body feels and the emotions that are surfacing.

Finally, take some time to reflect on what is in your direct control. Take time to notice how this feels. Then reflect on these questions:

- How many roles are you currently filling (within and outside of school)?
- What skills, gifts, and talents do I already have?
- What are the skills, knowledge, and insights I need in order to create change within myself and in my educational setting?
  - How and where will I gain them?
  - Who will help me?
- What boundaries are needed so that I am not depleting your precious resources?
- Who is my exhaustion serving?

After reflecting on all three levels: *care*, *influence*, and *control*, respond to these prompts:

- What is overwhelming me right now?
- Where would I like to (re)direct your energy and attention?
- What can I directly control each day?
- What will it feel like to be in more alignment with my values?

Even if you are not able to directly influence everything in the places you *care* about, that does not mean you are ineffective or "bad." It means that you are one person. This practice is very powerful to use with a group or a team within your school or school system. When you build out your lists together and see the webs of connection between all of the places you care about and can directly influence, you can build stronger efforts to challenge what needs to be changed. It also gives each of you some reprieve as you remember you do not need to do it all; the work can be distributed and shared across many people.

Depending on your level of influence and power within the system (from Chapter 7), you may have more pull than someone else. Even if you do not have a high level of power and influence, the way you show up matters. We may not be able to completely change the system, and we cannot change anyone else, but we do have some control over how we show up.

- Who inspires me?
- Who and what refills my cup?
- Whose support can help me sustain momentum?
- What would that support look like for me?
- What are habits that are contributing to my stress that I have control over (e.g. checking email constantly, media consumption, etc.)?
- How can I ensure I stay well as I work toward disrupting policies and practices that make us unwell?
- How can I ensure that other people are well as they work toward disrupting policies and practices that make us unwell?
- How do I want to disrupt harm while simultaneously creating room for healing?
- What is getting in the way of engaging in this work within myself and across our organization?
    - What is in my realm of control?

After this reflection, move around and take some time away from formally reflecting for at least 5 minutes. Then reread your reflections and write out a plan of action.

Asking the More Beautiful Question

Change is happening all the time in our schools and school systems. We, as individuals, are changing all the time. As we discussed in Chapter 7, far too often changes that are made come from top-down mandates rather than built with the people impacted by those decisions. Learning to embrace change takes our whole selves: mind, body, and heart. The clearer we are on *what* needs to change and *why* for ourselves, the easier it is to clearly communicate the change-purpose to others. When we are clear on *what* we are working toward (e.g. justice, healing), we can be open and receptive to multiple paths toward justice and healing.

While it is alluring to be so committed to change and determined that we know exactly what needs to get done, we must also learn to be adaptive and responsive through our collaboration with others. As we have explored throughout this book, we cannot embark on changework as a solo endeavor. We need to remember that our way is *a* way, but it is not *the* way. One path of finding what is blocking our path toward changing culture, habits, and practices is to ask beautiful questions.

It is important to be aware of the energy you are holding when posing these questions. If you can harness a very grounded and innerly connected nervous system while asking these questions, they will be experienced differently by the person or people receiving them. It doesn't guarantee they will respond in ways you hope, but it does mean you are more likely to leave the space feeling clear that you did what you could do from a space of love and integrity.

This is the way we do things.
Why?
It has always been this way.
Is it working?

I don't see it not working.
Who is it working for?
Well, most people find it good/fun.
That is true, some people do. But who is it not working for?
I hadn't thought of that.
What could we do to change what we're doing?
I'm not sure.
Who could help us figure this out?
Maybe the students.
Who else?
Families and community members.
Who else?
People within our schools.
What would we ask them?
How can our schools become sites of healing and justice?
That is the more beautiful question.

Appendix: Notes on Introducing Mindfulness to Others

Before Teaching Others

As mentioned in Chapter 1, it is important to practice these mindfulness-based practices before teaching them to others. As you practice in different settings and in different emotional states, you will get a sense of your own experiences with these practices and this will help you develop your own way of explaining them. It also helps to build inner compassion and external compassion. You'll notice that sometimes your mind wanders or your attention is too scattered to settle quickly. That insight may help you find a little more patience when you notice other people, adults and/or youth, fidgeting or opting out of the practice you're leading.

While mindfulness-based practices do have abundant research into their value and benefit, it is essential to ensure that they are used with a trauma-informed and culturally-responsive/culturally-sustaining approach (Dhaliwal, 2016; Howard et al., 2020; Ladson-Billings, 2021). There are many reasons why some mindfulness practices may be uncomfortable for someone. It is not necessary for someone (or for you) to explain themselves about why a certain practice is uncomfortable. As Alex Shevrin Venet notes, we do not need to be a "trauma detective" in order to be trauma-informed (Venet 2019). There are many reasons why mindfulness practices should always be optional and not mandated.

As mentioned in the first chapter, focusing on the breath may not feel calming for some people. Breathing practices might sometimes be helpful; other times, they may not. For some people a body scan will not feel comfortable. Their discomfort might be connected to medical trauma or other body-based harm they experienced. As discussed in Chapter 1, a body scan is probably not something to practice in a school setting unless full consent has been received. There may be cultural and/or religious reasons why people opt out or choose to modify practices. Allowing ample room for difference in people's experiences and participation with these practices is trauma-informed and culturally-sustaining.

Mindfulness practices should never have required participation. It may seem like students or a colleague would benefit from these practices, but they must have a choice about if, when, and how they engage in any practice. We do not get to decide what is good for someone else regardless of our research, knowledge, experience, position of authority or expertise as has been discussed throughout the book.

A trauma-informed approach to teaching mindfulness practices allows for choice and agency. No matter who your audience is, youth or adults, everyone has the right to opt out. This should always be shared at the beginning, prior to starting. I often tell people: "If you start feeling overwhelmed just tune me out. You can replay a song you love in your head or think about whatever it is you want to think about."

There should always be alternatives offered, such as drawing or doodling, during the time when other people may be engaged in a different mindfulness activity. Drawing and doodling are also supportive practices that can soothe overstimulated nervous systems.

Whenever you introduce a practice, be aware of accessibility. Think about how you can modify and adapt practices to ensure there is an access point for all of your participants, whether adults or youth. You may need to ask for input from others and/or solicit feedback about what worked or didn't work.

Remind students that everyone's practice will look and feel different. Some people may find breathing very relaxing while others may find it overwhelming. The same practice might feel very different from one session to the next. Activities that may be upregulating and energizing for some people may prove downregulating and relaxing for others. The idea that everyone should be doing the same thing in the same way is not responsive to a wide variety of preferences and needs in any group of people, so it is essential to shift out of the idea that one-practice-works-for-everyone.

A crucial part of creating culturally-responsive and neuro-affirming spaces means that there is never an effort to force people to all act in the same way. One time when I facilitated a group of my peers and taught deep listening, I encouraged people to sit facing each other. During the whole-group debrief, one of my peers reflected that in their culture, it was considered rude, or even threatening, to make direct eye contact with someone for a long period of time. Around the same time, I saw a video of a student saying "I can either look at you or I can listen to you but I can't do both." These were both essential reminders that eye contact is not a universal truth that everyone must adhere to; individuals experience it in different ways. Some people find that looking at someone's face can be too overstimulating; they become distracted by facial expressions and movements. With these pieces of information, I have completely shifted the way I teach deep listening with adults and youth.

Allow room for people to be uncomfortable. People's discomfort will present differently. Sometimes people will be giggly or silly. Other people may harrumph, but will do the practice anyway. Avoid the temptation to require that people are completely serious. It will take the joy out of the practices.

Before starting a practice, share as much information as is needed about the practice you are introducing. It is important that you are also modeling the practice. This creates a space in which you, as a teacher or a leader, are embodying what you are asking of other people and leads to trustworthiness. Putting youth in leadership roles can also support these practices.

For all of these practices, ask your participants to try to do these silently (or as quietly as they can; there are always giggles that erupt during these practices—something which always brings me joy). These can be used as short reset moments when you notice there is a lot of pent-up energy and/or bored energy.

Do not require that anyone close their eyes. This can be too overwhelming. Offer the option to close your eyes or focus your eyes somewhere on the floor, your desk, the wall, outside the window, etc. Just remind people to not stare at each other; this will inevitably create giggles and/or awkwardness – or both!

I suggest asking people to check in with how they feel (what's their level of energy, what emotions they are feeling) prior to the practice and then asking them to check in with how they feel after. You can share with them that taking note of how we feel before and after can help us make observations about our internal states and understand how practices impact us.

Not all people feel fully safe at work or in school. They may have an underlying sense of un-ease or hypervigilance. We cannot force—or try to intellectually convince—someone they are safe. This is especially true for anyone who has experienced bullying, harassment, or any other work and/or school-based harm. It is important to recognize who does and who does not feel safe and to work with them, their support network (i.e. family members/caring adults in a student's life), and your school-based team to build/rebuild safety.

Working with youth and/or your colleagues/team/staff in co-creating and co-designing the when/where/and how of mindfulness practices will have a large impact. Rather than mindfulness practices being something that is *done to*, or done for the "good of others", which is rooted in saviorism mentality, they become practices the community creates together. A collaborative approach in which people are both acting as students and teachers reduces power imbalances (Freire 2018; hooks 1994).

Youth are incredibly skilled at connecting with each other and supporting each other in ways adults just cannot. Creating opportunities for youth to teach each other can be very impactful. It may be helpful to create leadership opportunities for students. Be cognizant of *which* students are entrusted with leadership positions as we discussed in the chapter on biases.

Remember, it is critical to have your own personal mindfulness practice before teaching anyone else. It is also necessary to frequently remind ourselves that just because something works for us doesn't mean it will work well for others. Conversely, just because we dislike a certain practice doesn't mean others won't enjoy it. Taking ourselves too seriously when teaching others or believing that students must take these practices as seriously as we are, will only hinder participation. It will also increase the likelihood of experiencing frustration. Flexibility, creativity, responsiveness, humor, and curiosity are antidotes to trying to perfect mindfulness.

References

Adams, M., & Zúñiga, X. (2016). Getting Started: Core Concepts for Reaching Social Justice Education. In *Teaching for Diversity and Social Justice* (3rd ed., pp. 95–130). Routledge.

Agarwal, P. (2021). *Sway: Unravelling Unconscious Bias*. Bloomsbury Publishing.

Ahmed, M. A. O., Zhang, J., Fouad, A. S., Mousa, K., & Nour, H. M. (2024). The Dark Side of Leadership: How Toxic Leadership Fuels Counterproductive Work Behaviors through Organizational Cynicism and Injustice. *Sustainability*, 17(1), 105.

Akhavan, N., Walsh, N., & Goree, J. (2021). Benefits of Mindfulness Professional Development for Elementary Teachers: Considerations for District and School-level Leaders. *Journal of School Administration Research and Development*, 6(1), 24–42. https://doi.org/10.32674/jsard.v6i1.2462

Alessandra, T., & O'Connor, M. J. (1996). *The Platinum Rule*. Warner Books.

Almengor, R. A. (2020). Women Colorizing Restorative Practice in White-Led Institutions. In Edward C. Valandra & Waŋbli W. Hokšíla (Ed.), *Colorizing Restorative Justice: Voicing Our Realities* (pp. 131–141). Living Justice Press.

Amemiya, J., Mortenson, E., & Wang, M.-T. (2020). Minor Infractions are Not Minor: School Infractions for Minor Misconduct May Increase Adolescents' Defiant Behavior and Contribute to Racial Disparities in School Discipline. *The American Psychologist*, 75(1), 23–36.

American Civil Liberties Union. (2019, February 27). Letter to the House Committee on Education and Labor on Restraint and Seclusion in Schools. *American Civil Liberties Union*. https://www.aclu.org/documents/letter-house-committee-education-and-labor-restraint-and-seclusion-schools

Anastasiou, S. (2025). Counteracting Toxic Leadership in Education: Transforming Schools through Emotional Intelligence and Ethical Leadership. *Administrative Sciences*, 15(8), 312.

Annamma, S. A. (2018). *The Pedagogy of Pathologization: Dis/abled Girls of Color in the School–Prison Nexus*. Routledge.

Annamma, S. A., Connor, D. J., & Ferri, B. A. (2016). Dis/ability Critical Race Studies (DisCrit): Theorizing at the Intersections of Race and Dis/Ability. In D. J. Connor, B. A. Ferri, & S. A. Annamma (Eds.), *DisCrit: Disability Studies and Critical Race Theory in Education* (pp. 9–32). Teachers College Press.

Avant, D. W. (2011). Unwrapping Tradition: Shifting from Traditional Leadership to Transformative Action. In C. M. Shields (Ed.), *Transformative Leadership: A Reader* (pp. 114–127). Peter Lang.

Bal, A., Kozleski, E. B., Schrader, E. M., Rodriguez, E. M., & Pelton, S. (2014). Systemic Transformation from the Ground-Up. *Remedial and Special Education: RASE*, 35(6), 327–339.

Bal, P. M., & Veltkamp, M. (2013). How Does Fiction Reading Influence Empathy? An Experimental Investigation on the Role of Emotional Transportation. *PloS One*, 8(1), e55341.

Baldwin, J., & Giovanni, N. (1973). *A Dialogue*. B. Lippincott & Co.

Ballotpedia. (2022). *Analysis of School District and Board Member Characteristics, 2022*. Ballotpedia. https://ballotpedia.org/Analysis_of_school_district_and_board_member_characteristics,_2022

Barrett, L. F. (2004). Feelings or Words? Understanding the Content in Self-report Ratings of Experienced Emotion. *Journal of Personality and Social Psychology*, 87(2), 266–281.

Barrett, L. F. (2017). *How Emotions are Made: The Secret Life of the Brain*. Pan Macmillan.

Barrett, L. F., Gross, J., Christensen, T. C., & Benvenuto, M. (2001). Knowing What You're Feeling and Knowing What to Do About It: Mapping the Relation between Emotion Differentiation and Emotion Regulation. *Cognition and Emotion*, 15(6), 713–724.

Baum, B. (2006). *The Rise and Fall of the Caucasian Race: A Political History of Racial Identity*. NYU Press.

Bell, C. (2015). The Hidden Side of Zero Tolerance Policies: The African American Perspective. *Sociology Compass*, 9(1), 14–22.

Bell, J. (2018a). Understanding Adultism: A Key to Developing Positive Youth-Adult Relationships. In M. Adams, W. J. Blumenfeld, D. Chase J. Catalano, K. "Safire" DeJong, H. W. Hackman, L. E. Hopkins, B. J. Love, M. L. Peter, D. Shlasko, and X. Zúñiga (Eds.), *Readings for Diversity and Social Justice* (4th ed., pp. 553–555). Routledge.

Bell, L. (2018b). Theoretical Foundations for Social Justice Education. In M. Adams, W. J. Blumenfeld, D. C. J. Catalano, K. "Safire" DeJong, H. W. Hackman, L. E. Hopkins, B. J. Love, M. L. Peters, D. Shlasko, & X. Zúñiga (Eds.), *Readings and Teachings for Diversity and Social Justice* (4th ed., pp. 21–44). Routledge.

Benko, G. (2023). The Effects of Cross-cultural Relationships on Society. *Canadian Journal of Family and Youth / Le Journal Canadien de Famille et de La Jeunesse*, 15(2), 44–53.

Beyer, S. V. (2016). *Talking Stick*. Bear & Company.

Bloom, S. L., & Farragher, B. (2013). *Restoring Sanctuary: A New Operating System for Trauma-Informed Systems of Care*. OUP.

Brach, T. (2004). *Radical Acceptance*. Bantam.

Brock, R. N., & Lettini, G. (2012). *Soul Repair*. Beacon Press.

Brown, B. (2013, January 14). *Shame vs. Guilt*. https://brenebrown.com/articles/2013/01/15/shame-v-guilt/

Brown, B. (2018). *Dare to Lead: Brave Work. Tough Conversations. Whole Hearts*. Random House.

Brown, B. (2020, July 1). Brené Brown on Shame and Accountability. Unlocking Us. https://brenebrown.com/podcast/brene-on-shame-and-accountability/

Brown, B. (2022). *Atlas of the Heart*. Diversified Publishing.

Butts, H. F. (2002). The Black Mask of Humanity: Racial/ethnic Discrimination and Post-traumatic Stress Disorder. *The Journal of the American Academy of Psychiatry and the Law*, 30(3), 336–339.

Cao, Q., Xiang, H., Wang, Y., Liu, F., Weng, X., & Xu, F. (2025). Negative Impact of Insufficient Sleep on the Brain. *Brain-Apparatus Communication: A Journal of Bacomics*, 4(1). https://doi.org/10.1080/27706710.2025.2465538

Chambers, C. (2025). What a New Survey Says about Teachers' Plans to Leave Their Jobs. https://www.nea.org/nea-today/all-news-articles/what-new-survey-says-about-teachers-plans-leave-their-jobs

Chamorro-Premuzic, T. (2019). *Why Do So Many Incompetent Men Become Leaders?: (And How to Fix It)*. Harvard Business Press.

Chapman, B. P., Fiscella, K., Kawachi, I., Duberstein, P., & Muennig, P. (2013). Emotion Suppression and Mortality Risk Over a 12-year Follow-up. *Journal of Psychosomatic Research*, 75(4), 381–385.

Chemaly, S. (2018). *Rage Becomes Her: The Power of Women's Anger*. Simon and Schuster.

Coates, T.-N. (2017). *Ta-Nehisi Coates on words that don't belong to everyone | We Were Eight Years In Power Book Tour* [Video]. YouTube. https://www.youtube.com/watch?v=QO15S3WC9pg

Collins, P. H. (2015). Intersectionality's Definitional Dilemmas. *Annual Review of Sociology*, 41(1), 1–20.

Covey, S. R. (2020). *The 7 Habits of Highly Effective People*. Simon & Schuster.

Crenshaw, K., Gotanda, N., Peller, G., & Thomas, K. (1995). *Critical Race Theory: The Key Writings that Formed the Movement*. The New Press.

Dean, W., Talbot, S., & Dean, A. (2019). Reframing Clinician Distress: Moral Injury Not Burnout. *Federal Practitioner: For the Health Care Professionals of the VA, DoD, and PHS*, 36(9), 400–402.

Dhaliwal, K. (2016, October 24). Racing ACEs Gathering and Reflection: If It's Not Racially Just, It's Not Trauma-informed. *ACEs Too High*. https://acestoohigh.com/2016/10/24/racing-aces-gathering-and-reflection-if-its-not-racially-just-its-not-trauma-informed/

Diaz, J. (2015). Kicked Out! Unfair and Unequal Student Discipline in Vermont's Public Schools. Retrieved from State of Vermont Human Rights Commission website: https://www.vtlegalaid.org/sites/vtlegalaid/files/publications/Kicked-Out-Unfair-Unequal-Student-Discipline-Vermont-Public-Schools-%28limited-accessibility%29.pdf

Diniz, G., Korkes, L., Tristão, L. S., Pelegrini, R., Bellodi, P. L., & Bernardo, W. M. (2023). The Effects of Gratitude Interventions: A Systematic Review and Meta-analysis. *Einstein* (Sao Paulo, Brazil), 21, eRW0371.

Duane, A. (2023). School-Based Trauma: A Scoping Review. *Journal of Trauma Studies in Education*, 2(2), 102–124.

Dulfano, I. (2018). Anzaldúa: Authentic Leadership and Indigenous Feminism in XXIst Century. *Camino Real*, 13(10).

Eberhardt, J. L. (2020). *Biased: Uncovering the Hidden Prejudice That Shapes What We See, Think, and Do*. Penguin.

Edmondson, A. (1999). Psychological Safety and Learning Behavior in Work Teams. *Administrative Science Quarterly*, 44(2), 350–383.

ethos. (2025a). Oxford Dictionary. December 15, 2025. Retrieved from https://www.oed.com/?tl=true

ethos. (2025b). In Merriam-Webster.com. Retrieved December 15, 2025, from https://www.merriam-webster.com/dictionary/hacker

Fadus, M. C., Ginsburg, K. R., Sobowale, K., Halliday-Boykins, C. A., Bryant, B. E., Gray, K. M., & Squeglia, L. M. (2020). Unconscious Bias and the Diagnosis of Disruptive Behavior Disorders and ADHD in African

American and Hispanic Youth. *Academic Psychiatry: The Journal of the American Association of Directors of Psychiatric Residency Training and the Association for Academic Psychiatry*, 44(1), 95–102.

Farinas, C. (2016, April 22). 4 Ways Ableism in My Elementary School Left Me Completely Traumatized. *Everyday Feminism*. https://everydayfeminism.com/2016/04/ableism-elementary-school/

Fowler, Z., Law, K. F., & Gaesser, B. (2021). Against Empathy Bias: The Moral Value of Equitable Empathy. *Psychological Science*, 32(5), 766–779.

Freire, P. (2018). *Pedagogy of the Oppressed* (50th Anniversary ed.). Bloomsbury Publishing USA.

Gaffney, C. (2019). *When Schools Cause Trauma*. Learning for Justice.

Gilliam, W. S., Maupin, A. N., Reyes, C. R., Accavitti, M., & Shic, F. (2016). *Do Early Educators' Implicit Biases Regarding Sex Race Relate Behavior Expectations Recommendations Preschool Expulsions Suspensions?* Yale University Child Study Center.

Goldstein, E., Topitzes, J., Miller-Cribbs, J., & Brown, R. L. (2021). Influence of Race/Ethnicity and Income on the Link between Adverse Childhood Experiences and Child Flourishing. *Pediatric Research*, 89(7), 1861–1869.

Gordon, A. M., Impett, E. A., Kogan, A., Oveis, C., & Keltner, D. (2012). To Have and to Hold: Gratitude Promotes Relationship Maintenance in Intimate Bonds. *Journal of Personality and Social Psychology*, 103(2), 257–274.

Gorski, P. C. (2015). Relieving Burnout and the "Martyr Syndrome" among Social Justice Education Activists: The Implications and Effects of Mindfulness. *The Urban Review*, 47(4), 696–716. https://doi.org/10.1007/s11256-015-0330-0

Gorski, P. C., & Chen, C. (2015). "Frayed All Over:" The Causes and Consequences of Activist Burnout Among Social Justice Education Activists. *Educational Studies*, 51(5), 385–405.

Gower, T., Pham, J., Jouriles, E. N., Rosenfield, D., & Bowen, H. J. (2022). Cognitive Biases in Perceptions of Posttraumatic Growth: A Systematic Review and Meta-analysis. *Clinical Psychology Review*, 94(102159), 102159.

Hackman, R. (2023). *Emotional Labor: The Invisible Work Shaping Our Lives and How to Claim Our Power*. Flatiron Books.

Haga, K. (2020). *Healing Resistance: A Radically Different Response to Harm*. Parallax Press.

Haines, S. K. (2019). *The Politics of Trauma: Somatics, Healing, and Social Justice*. North Atlantic Books.

Hanh, T. N. (2007, September 20). *What Is Mindfulness?* Plum Village. https://plumvillage.org/library/clips/what-is-mindfulness

Hanh, T. N. (2017). *How to Fight*. Parallax Press.

Harro, B. (2018). The Cycle of Socialization. In M. Adams, W. J. Blumenfeld, D. C. J. Catalano, K. "Safire" DeJong, H. W. Hackman, L. E. Hopkins, B. J. Love, M. L. Peters, D. Shlasko, and X. Zúñiga (Eds.), *Readings for Diversity and Social Justice* (4th ed., pp. 27–33). Routledge.

Hartling, L. M., Rosen, W., Walker, M., & Jordan, J. V. (2000). *Shame Humiliation: From Isolation Relational Transformation*. Wellesley College.

Hersey, T. (2022). *Rest Is Resistance: A Manifesto*. Hachette UK.

Hirshberg, M. J., Davidson, R. J., & Goldberg, S. B. (2023). Educators Are Not Alright: Mental Health During COVID-19. *Educational Researcher*, 52(1), 48–52.

Ho, J. A. (2015). *Racial Ambiguity in Asian American Culture*. Rutgers University Press.

Hofmann, S. G., Grossman, P., & Hinton, D. E. (2011). Loving-kindness and Compassion Meditation: Potential for Psychological Interventions. *Clinical Psychology Review*, 31(7), 1126–1132.

hooks, b. (1994). *Teaching to Transgress: Education as the Practice of Freedom*. Routledge. https://doi.org/10.4324/9780203700280

hooks, b. (2000). *Feminism Is for Everybody*. South End Press.

hooks, b. (2001). *All About Love: New Visions*. HarperCollins.

hooks, b. (2004). *The Will to Change: Men, Masculinity, and Love*. Simon and Schuster.

hooks, b. (2010). Understanding Patriarchy. https://theanarchistlibrary.org/library/bell-hooks-understanding-patriarchy

hooks, b. (2013, November 11). Black Female Voices: Who Is Listening – A Public Dialogue between bell hooks + Melissa Harris-Perry [Video]. https://www.youtube.com/watch?v=5OmgqXao1ng&t=4s. The New School.

Houston, D. M., & Hartney, M. T. (2025, October 8). *Who's on Board? School Boards and Political Representation in an Age of Conflict*. Thomas B. Fordham Institute. https://fordhaminstitute.org/national/research/whos-board-school-boards-and-political-representation-age-conflict

Howard, J. R., Milner-McCall, T., & Howard, T. C. (2020). *No More Teaching Without Positive Relationships*. Heinemann.

Hülsheger, U. R., Alberts, H., Feinholdt, A., & Lang, J. W. B. (2013). Benefits of Mindfulness at Work: The Role of Mindfulness in Emotion Regulation, Emotional Exhaustion, and Job Satisfaction. *The Journal of Applied Psychology*, 98(2), 310–325. https://doi.org/10.1037/a0031313

Hurtado, A. (1996). *The Color of Privilege: Three Blasphemies on Race and Feminism*. University of Michigan Press.

Ighodaro, E., & Wiggan, G. A. (2009). *Curriculum Violence: America's New Civil Rights Issue*. Nova Science Publishers.

Johns Hopkins Medicine. (2025). *The Effects of Sleep Deprivation*. The Effects of Sleep Deprivation. https://www.hopkinsmedicine.org/health/wellness-and-prevention/the-effects-of-sleep-deprivation

Jones, F. (2020, April 5). *Who Has Power Over the System? (The Cycle of Systemic Exclusion)*. Liberate.ed. https://liberate-ed.com/2020/04/05/who-has-power-over-the-system-the-cycle-of-systemic-exclusion/

Jotkoff, E. (2022). NEA Survey: Massive Staff Shortages in Schools Leading to Educator Burnout; Alarming Number of Educators Indicating they Plan to Leave Profession. https://www.nea.org/about-nea/media-center/press-releases/nea-survey-massive-staff-shortages-schools-leading-educator

Jun, I. H. (2011). Transformative Leadership in a Diverse Setting. In C. M. Shields (Ed.), *Transformative Leadership: A Reader* (pp. 238–253). Peter Lang.

Kariou, A., Koutsimani, P., Montgomery, A., & Lainidi, O. (2021). Emotional Labor and Burnout among Teachers: A Systematic Review. *International Journal of Environmental Research and Public Health*, 18(23). https://doi.org/10.3390/ijerph182312760

Kashdan, T. B., Barrett, L. F., & McKnight, P. E. (2015). Unpacking Emotion Differentiation: Transforming Unpleasant Experience by Perceiving Distinctions in Negativity. *Current Directions in Psychological Science*, 24(1), 10–16.

Kent, D. (2024, September 24). Key Facts about Public School Teachers in the U.S. Pew Research Center. https://www.pewresearch.org/short-reads/2024/09/24/key-facts-about-public-school-teachers-in-the-u-s/

King, R. (2018). *Mindful of Race: Transforming Racism from the Inside Out*. Sounds True.

Kirk, G., & Okazawa-Rey, M. (2018). Identities and Social Locations: Who Am I? Who Are My People? In M. Adams, W. J. Blumenfeld, D. C. J. Catalano, K. "Safire" DeJong, H. W. Hackman, L. E. Hopkins, B. J. Love,

M. L. Peters, D. Shlasko, and X. Zúñiga (Eds.), *Readings for Diversity and Social Justice* (4th ed., pp. 10–15).

Knaus, C. B. (2018). "If Everyone Would Just Act White": Education as a Global Investment in Whiteness. *Whiteucation*. https://www.taylorfrancis.com/chapters/edit/10.4324/9781351253482-1/everyone-would-act-white-christopher-knaus

Knestrict, T. D. (2018). *Controlling Our Children: Hegemony and Deconstructing the Positive Behavioral Intervention Support Model*. Peter Lang.

Kotowski, S. E., Davis, K. G., & Barratt, C. L. (2022). Teachers Feeling the Burden of COVID-19: Impact on Well-being, Stress, and Burnout. *Work*, 71(2), 407–415.

Krause, A. J., Simon, E. B., Mander, B. A., Greer, S. M., Saletin, J. M., Goldstein-Piekarski, A. N., & Walker, M. P. (2017). The Sleep-deprived Human Brain. *Nature Reviews. Neuroscience*, 18(7), 404–418.

Kucinskas, J. (2019). *The Mindful Elite: Mobilizing from the Inside Out*. Oxford University Press.

Ladson-Billings, G. (2021). *Culturally Relevant Pedagogy: Asking a Different Question*. Teachers College Press.

Leiba, E. (2022). *I'm Not Yelling: A Black Woman's Guide to Navigating the Workplace*. Mango Media Inc.

Levine, P. A. (1997). *Waking The Tiger*. North Atlantic Books.

Levinson, M. (2015). Moral Injury and the Ethics of Educational Injustice. *Harvard Educational Review*, 85(2), 203–228.

Linehan, M. M. (1993). *Skills Training Manual for Treating Borderline Personality Disorder*. Guilford Publications.

Linklater, R. (2014). *Decolonizing Trauma Work: Indigenous Stories and Strategies*. Fernwood Publishing.

Lipsky, L. v. D., & Burke, C. (2009). *Trauma Stewardship: An Everyday Guide to Caring for Self While Caring for Others*. Berrett-Koehler Publishers.

Lisle-Johnson, T., & Kohli, R. (2020). Critical Black Women Educators: Resisting the Racial and Ideological Marginality of K–12 Teaching through Critical Professional Development. *Theory into Practice*, 59(4), 348–357.

Litz, B. T., Stein, N., Delaney, E., Lebowitz, L., Nash, W. P., Silva, C., & Maguen, S. (2009). Moral Injury and Moral Repair in War Veterans: A Preliminary Model and Intervention Strategy. *Clinical Psychology Review*, 29(0), 695–706.

Long, C. (2025). Poll Results: Stress and Burnout Pose Threat of Educator Shortages. *NeaToday*. https://www.nea.org/nea-today/all-news-articles/survey-says-were-crisis-point#:~:text=Some%2081%20percent%20of%20educators,source%20of%20job%2Drelated%20stress

Lorde, A. (2014). *Sister Outsider*. Crossing Press.

Love, B. L. (2019). *We Want to Do More Than Survive: Abolitionist Teaching and the Pursuit of Educational Freedom*. Beacon Press.

Magee, R. V. (2021). *The Inner Work of Racial Justice: Healing Ourselves and Transforming Our Communities Through Mindfulness*. Penguin.

Manne, K. (2020). Entitled: How Male Privilege Hurts Women. https://books.google.com/books?hl=en&lr=&id=kZDyDwAAQBAJ&oi=fnd&pg=PA3&dq=entitled+kate+manne&ots=5dqYzDlyck&sig=TABnNfMBMPTmOCxpz2rkoNZCspo

Maslach, C., & Leiter, M. P. (2016). Understanding the Burnout Experience: Recent Research and its Implications for Psychiatry. *World Psychiatry: Official Journal of the World Psychiatric Association (WPA)*, 15(2), 103–111.

Maslach, C., & Leiter, M. P. (2021, March 19). How to Measure Burnout Accurately and Ethically. *Harvard Business Review*. https://hbr.org/2021/03/how-to-measure-burnout-accurately-and-ethically

Matiz, A., Chiesa, A., D'Antoni, F., Barbieri, R., & Crescentini, C. (2025). Training for Mindfulness Teachers: Benefits for Mindfulness, Well-being, and Emotion Regulation. *Mindfulness* 16, 465–476. https://doi.org/10.1007/s12671-025-02520-z

McCombs, M., Scott, J., & Losen, D. J. (2022). Pushed Out: Trends and Disparities in Out-of-school Suspension. Learning Policy Institute. https://learningpolicyinstitute.org/product/crdc-school-suspension-report

Menakem, R. (2017). *My Grandmother's Hands: Racialized Trauma and the Pathway to Mending Our Hearts and Bodies*. Central Recovery Press.

Menge, C., & Gerick, J. (2026). The Potential of Transformational Leadership and Self-Regulation for Enhanced Occupational Well-being among Early-career Teachers. *Teaching and Teacher Education*, 169, 105238.

Merriam-Webster. (2025). Ethos. In Merriam-Webster.com dictionary. Retrieved December 15, 2025, from https://www.merriam-webster.com/dictionary/ethos

Morris, M. (2016). *Pushout: The Criminalization of Black Girls in Schools*. The New Press.

Murawski, M. (2020, July 30). *Leading Means Being More Human*. Art Museum Teaching. https://artmuseumteaching.com/2020/07/30/leading-means-being-more-human/

Nagoski, E., & Amelia Nagoski, D. M. A. (2020). *Burnout: The Secret to Unlocking the Stress Cycle*. Random House Publishing Group.

National Education Association et al. (2022). *Poll Results: Stress and Burnout Pose Threat of Educator Shortages*. National Education Association.

National Prevention Science Coalition. (2020, September 16). *Racially Disproportionate Discipline in Early Childhood Educational Settings*. NPSC. https://www.npscoalition.org/post/racially-disproportionate-discipline-in-early-childhood-educational-settings

Niemann, Y. F. (2012). Lessons from the Experiences of Women of Color Working in Academia. In G. Gutierrez y Muhs, Y. F. Niemann, C. G. Gonzalez, & A. P. Harris (Eds.), *Presumed Incompetent: The Intersections of Race and Class for Women in Academia* (pp. 446–499). University Press of Colorado.

Ogden, P. (2009). Emotion, Mindfulness, and Movement: Expanding the Regulatory Boundaries of the Window of Affect Tolerance. In D. Fosha, D. J. Siegel, & M. F. Solomon (Eds.), *The Healing Power of Emotion: Affective Neuroscience, Development & Clinical Practice* (pp. 204–231). W. W. Norton & Company.

Ogden, P., Pain, C., & Fisher, J. (2006). A Sensorimotor Approach to the Treatment of Trauma and Dissociation. *The Psychiatric Clinics of North America*, 29(1), 263–279, xi–xii.

Oxford Dictionary. (2025) Ethos. In Oxford English oed.com dictionary. Retrieved December 15, 2025, from https://www.oed.com/?tl=true

Painter, N. I. (2010). *The History of White People*. W. W. Norton & Company.

Pendharkar, E. (2022, October 20). Nearly Two-thirds of School Board Members Set to Step Down, Survey Finds. *Education Week*. https://www.edweek.org/leadership/more-than-a-third-of-school-board-members-set-to-step-down-survey-finds/2022/10

Petrovic, J., Mettler, J., Cho, S., & Heath, N. L. (2024). The Effects of Loving-kindness Interventions on Positive and Negative Mental Health Outcomes: A Systematic Review and Meta-analysis. *Clinical Psychology Review*, 110(102433), 102433.

Pierce, C. M., & Barbour, F. B. (Ed.) (1970). *The Black Seventies*. Porter Sargent.

Pipes, E. (2016). Legos and the 4 I's of Oppression. https://www.youtube.com/watch?v=3WWyVRo4Uas

Pizarro, M., & Kohli, R. (2020). "I Stopped Sleeping": Teachers of Color and the Impact of Racial Battle Fatigue. *Urban Education*, 55(7), 967–991.

Plummer, D. L., Stone, R. T., Powell, L., & Allison, J. (2016). Patterns of Adult Cross-racial Friendships: A Context for Understanding Contemporary Race Relations. *Cultural Diversity & Ethnic Minority Psychology*, 22(4), 479–494.

Poulin, M. J., Ministero, L. M., Gabriel, S., Morrison, C. D., & Naidu, E. (2021). Minding Your Own Business? Mindfulness Decreases Prosocial Behavior for People with Independent Self-construals. *Psychological Science*, 32(11), 1699–1708.

Purser, R. (2019). *McMindfulness: How Mindfulness Became The New Capitalist Spirituality*. Penguin Random House.

Quartana, P. J., & Burns, J. W. (2010). Emotion Suppression Affects Cardiovascular Responses to Initial and Subsequent Laboratory Stressors. *British Journal of Health Psychology*, 15(Pt 3), 511–528.

Real, T. (2022). *Us: Getting Past You and Me to Build a More Loving Relationship*. Goop Press/Rodale.

Rizkie, M. (2022). Effect Transformational Leadership School Principles, Quality Culture Job Satisfaction Teacher Performance. *International Journal of Social Science And Human Research*, 5(6), 2345–2353.

Robinson, O. P., Bridges, S. A., Rollins, L. H., & Schumacker, R. E. (2019). A Study of the Relation between Special Education Burnout and Job Satisfaction. *Journal of Research in Special Educational Needs: JORSEN*, 19(4), 295–303.

Russo, C., Danioni, F., Zagrean, I., & Barni, D. (2022). Changing Personal Values through Value-manipulation Tasks: A Systematic Literature Review Based on Schwartz's Theory of Basic Human Values. *European Journal of Investigation in Health Psychology and Education*, 12(7), 692–715.

Saleem, F. T., Anderson, R. E., & Williams, M. (2020). Addressing the "Myth" of Racial Trauma: Developmental and Ecological Considerations for Youth of Color. *Clinical Child and Family Psychology Review*, 23(1), 1–14.

Samaran, N. (2019). *Turn This World Inside Out: The Emergence of Nurturance Culture*. AK Press.

Sanchez, D. T., & Bonam, C. M. (2009). To Disclose or Not to Disclose Biracial Identity: The Effect of Biracial Disclosure on Perceiver Evaluations and Target Responses. *The Journal of Social Issues*, 65(1), 129–149.

Scott-Samuel, A. J. R., Crawshaw, P., & Oakley, A. (2015). "Men Behaving Badly": Patriarchy, Public Policy and Health Inequalities. *International Journal of Men's Health*, 14(3), 250–258.

Shah, V., & Grimaldos, D. (2022). Lies, Denials, and Cover-Ups: The Pervasiveness of Whiteness in School Districts Relations with Black and Racialized Parents. *Urban Education*, 59(6). https://doi.org/10.1177/00420859221095004

Shay, J. (1991). Learning About Combat Stress from Homer's Iliad. *Journal Traumatic Stress*, 4(4), 561–579.

Shields, C. M. (2004). Dialogic Leadership for Social Justice: Overcoming Pathologies of Silence. *Educational Administration Quarterly: EAQ*, 40(1), 109–132.

Shyman, E. (2016). The Reinforcement of Ableism: Normality, the Medical Model of Disability, and Humanism in Applied Behavior Analysis and ASD. *Intellectual and Developmental Disabilities*, 54(5), 366–376.

Siegel, D. J. (1999). *Developing Mind: Toward Neurobiology Interpersonal Experience*. Guilford Press.

Siegel, D. J., & Bryson, T. P. (2012). *The Whole-Brain Child: 12 Revolutionary Strategies to Nurture Your Child's Developing Mind*. Bantam.

Sieghart, M. A. (2022). *The Authority Gap: Why Women Are Still Taken Less Seriously Than Men, and What We Can Do About It*. W. W. Norton & Company.

Smidt, K. E., & Suvak, M. K. (2015). A Brief, But Nuanced, Review of Emotional Granularity and Emotion Differentiation Research. *Current Opinion in Psychology*, 3, 48–51. https://doi.org/10.1016/j.copsyc.2015.02.007

Sondel, B., Kretchmar, K., & Hadley Dunn, A. (2019). "Who Do These People Want Teaching Their Children?" White Saviorism, Colorblind Racism, and Anti-Blackness in "No Excuses" Charter Schools. *Urban Education*, 57(9), 1621–1650.

Srivastava, S., Tamir, M., McGonigal, K. M., John, O. P., & Gross, J. J. (2009). The Social Costs of Emotional Suppression: A Prospective Study of the Transition to College. *Journal of Personality and Social Psychology*, 96(4), 883–897.

Stanistreet, D., Bambra, C., & Scott-Samuel, A. (2005). Is Patriarchy the Source of Men's Higher Mortality? *Journal of Epidemiology and Community Health*, 59(10), 873–876.

Stephens, C. P. (2025, July 3). What the Research Says about School Boards: How Much Conflict Really is There? *Education Week*, 24–27.

Substance Abuse and Mental Health Services Administration. (2014). SAMHSA's Concept of Trauma and Guidance for a Trauma-informed Approach. https://calio.dspacedirect.org/handle/11212/1971

Sue, D. W. (2010). *Microaggressions in Everyday Life: Race, Gender, and Sexual Orientation*. John Wiley & Sons.

Sue, D. W. (2016). *Race Talk and the Conspiracy of Silence: Understanding and Facilitating Difficult Dialogues on Race*. John Wiley & Sons.

Tan, T. Y., Wachsmuth, L., & Tugade, M. M. (2022). Emotional Nuance: Examining Positive Emotional Granularity and Well-being. *Frontiers in Psychology*, 13, 715966.

Tatum, B. D. (2018). The Complexity of Identity: "Who Am I?" In M. Adams, W. J. Blumenfeld, C. Castañeda, H. Hackman, M. L. Peters, & X. Zúñiga (Eds.) *Readings for Diversity and Social Justice* (4th ed., pp. 7–9). Routledge.

Thom, K. C. (2022, April 5). *The Window of Transformation. Arise Embodiment; Kai Cheng Thom*. https://ariseembodiment.org/2022/04/05/the-window-of-transformation/

Thomas, K. M., Johnson-Bailey, J., Phelps, R. E., Tran, M. N., & Johnson, L. N. (2013). Women of Color at Midcareer: Going from Pet to Threat. In L. Comas-Diaz & B. Greene (Eds.), *Psychological Health of Women of Color: Intersections, Challenges, and Opportunities: Intersections, Challenges, and Opportunities* (pp. 275–286). ABC-CLIO.

Tootoosis, C. (2020, April 27). The Cunning of the Adult Supremacist. *Freedom Rising*. http://www.colbytootoosis.com/writings/adult-supremacy?fbclid=IwAR1-VTflJdnmLagwOemgBwT0dyEHo0rjc15jhlcrQ80Pd_4W9l1cq4uH5hk

Tutu, D., & Tutu, M. (2014). *The Book of Forgiving: The Fourfold Path for Healing Ourselves and Our World*. Harper One.

Vaid-Menon, A. (2020). *Beyond the Gender Binary*. Penguin.

Valenti, J., & Friedman, J. (2020). *Believe Me: How Trusting Women Can Change the World*. Basic Books.

VeneKlasen, L., & Miller, V. (Eds.). (2007). *A New Weave of Power, People and Politics*. Practical Action Publishing. https://doi.org/10.3362/9781780444208

Venet, A. S. (2019). Role-clarity and Boundaries for Trauma-informed Teachers. *Educational Considerations*, 44(2). https://doi.org/10.4148/0146-9282.2175

Venet, A. S. (2021). *Equity-Centered Trauma-Informed Education (Equity and Social Justice in Education)*. W. W. Norton & Company.

Volunteers of America. (2020, May 12). *Moral Injury: A Working Definition by Dr. Rita Brock*. Youtube. https://www.youtube.com/watch?v=XJtuUguqVVo

Voulgarides, C. K., Fergus, E., & King Thorius, K. A. (2017). Pursuing Equity: Disproportionality in Special Education and the Reframing of Technical Solutions to Address Systemic Inequities. *Review of Research in Education*, 41(1), 61–87. https://doi.org/10.3102/0091732x16686947

Willcox, G. (1982). The Feeling Wheel. *Transactional Analysis Journal*, 12(4), 274–276.

Wilson-Mendenhall, C. D., & Dunne, J. D. (2021). Cultivating Emotional Granularity. *Frontiers in Psychology*, 12, 703658.

Wiseman, T. (1996). A Concept Analysis of Empathy. *Journal of Advanced Nursing*, 23(6), 1162–1167.

Wolor, C. W., Ardiansyah, A., Rofaida, R., Nurkhin, A., & Rababah, M. A. (2022). Impact of Toxic Leadership on Employee Performance. *Health Psychology Research*, 10(4), 57551.

Wong, A. (2023, February 22). Learning How to Speak in the Language of Feelings: The Emotions Wheel. Somatopia.com. https://www.somatopia.com/blog/the-emotions-wheel-or-the-feelings-wheel

Wong, G., Sun, R., Adler, J., Yeung, K. W., Yu, S., & Gao, J. (2022). Loving-Kindness Meditation (LKM) Modulates Brain-heart Connection: An EEG Case Study. *Frontiers in Human Neuroscience*, 16, 891377.

Yoo, S. H., & Chung, J. (Eds.). (2010). *Expression Anger Across Cultures*. David Matsumoto.

Yudkin, D. A., Gantman, A. P., Hofmann, W., & Quoidbach, J. (2021). Binding Moral Values Gain Importance in the Presence of Close Others. *Nature Communications*, 12(1), 2718.

For Product Safety Concerns and Information please contact our EU
representative GPSR@taylorandfrancis.com
Taylor & Francis Verlag GmbH, Kaufingerstraße 24, 80331 München, Germany

www.ingramcontent.com/pod-product-compliance
Lightning Source LLC
LaVergne TN
LVHW010652110826
845149LV00014B/3057

* 9 7 8 1 0 3 2 8 7 1 1 7 2 *